WASHINGTON IRVING

A TRIBUTE

Edited by
Andrew B. Myers

SLEEPY HOLLOW RESTORATIONS

Tarrytown, New York

1972

817.2
I 27Yw
1972

ILLUS. 2—*Washington Irving, daguerreotype by Matthew Brady*

CONTENTS

ILLUSTRATIONS

Chapter Illustrations
by
Felix O. C. Darley (1822-1888)
Published by The American Art Union
New York, 1848-1849

PREFACE

In the early fall of 1820 the seventh and final "Part" of *The Sketch Book of Geoffrey Crayon, Gent.* was published in this country. This event was paralleled by publication in England of the second of two bound collections of the separate parts.

In October 1970, to celebrate the sesquicentennial of *The Sketch Book,* Sleepy Hollow Restorations, of Tarrytown, New York, arranged for a "Washington Irving Symposium." It was especially fitting that this organization be host on this anniversary occasion, for among the historic properties it has preserved and offers to the twentieth-century public is Sunnyside, Irving's pre-Civil War home, on grounds overlooking the Hudson River in Tarrytown, New York. The direction of the program was chiefly undertaken by Professor Jacob Judd, Executive Officer of the Department of History at Lehman College of the City University of New York, and Research Consultant to Sleepy Hollow Restorations. The meeting itself was at another Sleepy Hollow Restorations historic restoration, colonial Philipsburg Manor, Upper Mills, North Tarrytown. Eight panelists participated, each invited for particular expertise in some aspect of the many worlds of Washington Irving, the man and the artist.

For this commemorative volume the editor has, with

permission, somewhat reordered the sequence of papers, and made minor textual changes, chiefly to avoid repetition of the numerous original cross-references to the specific schedule of events. An Introduction has been added to outline Irving's career so that *The Sketch Book* and "Geoffrey Crayon, Gent." may be seen in full context. The first four papers as here printed focus on Irving's achievements in *The Sketch Book* itself and on the age it reflected and influenced. The next four widen the scope of commentary to include other important aspects of his long life and transatlantic reputation.

Taken together, they offer a thoughtful, if necessarily limited, and a congratulatory, if often candid, account of Washington Irving's literary labors and life style, a century and a half after he began *The Sketch Book's* first unit of miscellaneous prose pieces with his own brief, easygoing, but elegantly turned-out "Author's Account of Himself."

Andrew B. Myers
October 1971

INTRODUCTION

Andrew B. Myers

For all its seemingly youthful spirit and open sentiment *The Sketch Book* (1819-1820) was not a young man's book, nor its author's first success. Washington Irving, born in New York City on April 3, 1783, as our Revolution was ending, and even named by his Scottish-English immigrant parents for their patriot hero General George Washington, was by the time he created "Geoffrey Crayon, Gent." well into his thirties. Behind him was some fifteen years of amateur quill-driving, which if often imaginative and promising, still added up to but a long apprenticeship in belles lettres, and was far from a total commitment to a determined career as an American man of letters.

For that matter no one else in the new United States had yet dared to gamble everything on such a chancy way of life *and* stay with it. Philip Freneau had tried it as poet and tasted bitter defeat. Charles Brockden Brown had tried it as novelist and turned aside, even before his early death. Periodical journalists and polemical versifiers there were aplenty, but of successful professionals, especially in the British sense, there were none, even as the second decade of the new century opened. The plain fact is, including the very uncertain economics of authorship,

1

that whatever talents were available, the time was not yet ripe for such a luxury. The nation had more hard-headed and utilitarian business to accomplish first. Our indigenous fine arts, including literature, long remained derivative and parochial, tentative and unsure. Political independence we had—yes; but cultural independence—no! It was Washington Irving, and with *The Sketch Book* before anything else, who made the first real break-through in letters, but it came comparatively late, both for the man himself and for his waiting contemporaries, as readers and as critics.

As fledgling author Irving had dabbled in the essay with a series of papers printed during 1802-1803 in a short-lived New York City periodical *The Morning Chronicle*. Edited and published together as *Letters of Jonathan Oldstyle, Gent.*, they are today little more than a bibliographer's puzzle, except for the intimate views they give of the boisterous American theater of the day. Even then Irving showed a passion for stage performances of all kinds, and remained a theater buff for the rest of his long life.

With "Jonathan Oldstyle," warts and all, he proved if only in personal satisfaction that this kind of ephemeral prose writing was to his liking. Over the years 1807-1808, in collaboration with his crony James Kirke Paulding and his older brother William Irving, he helped produce *Salmagundi; Or, The Whim-Whams And Opinions Of Launcelot Langstaff, & Others.* This is a rambunctious collection of gossipy essays, tales within tales, and light verse, occasionally laced, as an innocent punch can be with profit, by a tot of more potent—and here literary—spirits. It was clearly a New York product, even in the days before "Knickerbocker" was coined as a term to characterize this already bustling and cosmopolitan center.

About the turn of the century this Atlantic port city, latterly also the federal capital, had a population of some seventy thousand of widely mixed origins, although the country as a whole was rather homogeneous. And just as this early New York City was commercially busy so it was, in a further sense, intellectually active, though still without much direction, in the arts at least. Conversation among its restless citizens was often quick and clever, if rarely profound. A sharp sense of humor had developed locally, pairing a kind of inherited eighteenth-century wit that was obviously English in origin, and somewhat cynical, with a broader sense of fun which was decidedly North American, and colonial, in origin.

But for all its potential largeness and increasing sophistication, the young Irving's Manhattan and its environs still deserved only a small dot on the world's map. Inevitably it had a share of small-town mentality since even in the first of the 1800s open country was not remarkably far away. Henry Adams would write in 1889 as historian, and with his own Boston and Massachusetts as frames of reference, "New York was still a frontier state, and although the city was European in its age and habits, travelers needed to go few miles from the Hudson to find a wilderness like that of Ohio and Tennessee."[1]

This temporary frontier line would move on, especially after Governor George Clinton's "ditch," the Erie Canal, was opened in the 1820s, but long since, one permanent impression on the home town of our attorney-about-town and nascent author Mr. Washington Irving, Esq., had been its Dutch colonial inheritance. By the early nineteenth century surprisingly much was still left, though not untouched by time, of the artifacts and traditions of New Amsterdam, as well as in the surrounding Hudson River Valley area. Van Wyck Brooks in 1944 wrote of the city of Irving's early manhood:

> Even in New York there were still many Dutch-built houses, with gables facing the street and crow-stepped roofs, especially in the Bowery, a dusty country road that was lined with quaint Dutch cottages, surrounded by gardens. Many of the older families kept up their trade with Holland, proud of their associations with the Dutch republic and the

memory of Grotius and DeWitt, and their houses were crammed with high-backed chairs, oaken cabinets and old Dutch paintings, while they spoke the tongue of New Amsterdam both in church and market.[2]

Small wonder then that with his inquisitiveness, natural sense of fun, and growing antiquarian interest in the past, Irving would in time turn to this colonial Dutch tradition for inspiration. The result in 1809 was a straight-faced spoof of New Netherland's seventeenth-century governors and their subjects, *A History of New York . . . By Diedrich Knickerbocker,* which was begun as a parody of a recent dull guidebook, carried on more seriously as a satire even of contemporary events, and became in sum an American masterpiece of comic history. The combination of fact and fiction was at once, especially for readers whose ancestors were not Netherlanders, a howling success. The cliché can stand as the simple truth. Overseas Walter Scott could remember reading the book to his family and laughing till his sides were sore.

Rather rushed into print in the offhand manner of the dilettante its author still was, the book was nevertheless cleverly presented to the public in an advertising hoax. Fictitious newspaper items were planted to help make credible the "Diedrich Knickerbocker" who was supposedly author of the manuscript. Little could the creator of the "small, brisk-looking old gentleman, dressed in a rusty black coat, a pair of olive velvet breeches, and a small cocked hat" have guessed what a long and dramatic life his new alter ego was destined to have. Indeed, like Rip Van Winkle after him, Diedrich soon stepped out of Irving's pages to take on a life of his own. The book, whatever the impudence in places, and the harmless fabrications in others, launched the word "Knickerbocker" as a synonym for New Yorker. On revising the book forty years later Irving would express amazement that "Knickerbocker" had "become a 'household word,' used to give the home stamp to everything recommended for popular acceptation, such as Knickerbocker societies, Knickerbocker insurance companies, Knickerbocker steamboats, Knickerbocker omnibuses, Knickerbocker bread, and Knickerbocker ice." He could even see about him "New Yorkers of Dutch descent priding themselves upon being "genuine Knickerbockers." And we ourselves can see that Irving's make-believe character in one form flourishes still as "Father Knickerbocker," a symbol for New York City itself.

In 1815, by now past thirty, and, after the death of his young sweetheart Matilda Hoffman, still single and unsettled in place or profession, he sailed for Liverpool to help out the Irving family import firm in a time of international postwar financial crisis. Neither his own unaccustomed counting house efforts nor aught else prevailed, and the embarrassment of bankruptcy followed in 1818, effectively cutting off brother Washington from occupation and anticipated income. What to do? Forced to stare an uncertain future in the face, he opted to capitalize on the one talent he was sure he had—writing.

Though in the end Irving never came close to the degradation of the proverbial Grub Street hack, he had to live through some dark hours in London lodgings. If he were really to succeed, without deliberately limiting himself to the horizons of the struggling arts in the United States, he had sooner or later to conquer the imperial capital on the Thames, in competition with a host of native Romantic stalwarts. As Professor Woodring's paper in this collection shows, these were tense times for the British body politic, here in the heyday of the master of fiction Scott, and of the poets Byron, Shelley, and Keats, and essayists like Hazlitt and Lamb. This was an enormous challenge for a mere American. In the same year of complete publication of *The Sketch Book*, the critic Sydney Smith, writing in the vaunted *Edinburgh Review*, felt free to say: "In all the four quarters of the globe who reads an American book, or goes to an American play? or looks at an American picture or statue?" The answer, as often has been said and with justice, came from that expatriate Knickerbocker man of letters Washington Irving, who, both by design and dumb luck, had just seen into print "Geoffrey Crayon's" unforeseen best seller.

By design, between May 1819 and September 1820, some sixteen months, the seven separate "Parts" of *The Sketch Book* were produced in this country, in paper wrappers, and published in four seaboard cities at irregular intervals of two or three months. The complete work was turned out in New York City by a printer on Greenwich Street with the real name of C. S. Van Winkle. He had been contacted for "Wash" by those self-taught literary agents, an older brother, Ebenezer Irving, and a boyhood friend, Henry Brevoort. The author periodically mailed them his bundles of manuscript from Britain — diffident not only about trying for success initially in London, but even about putting his true name on the title page. In such hesitations, but as it turned out, as a perfect artistic disguise, was born "Geoffrey Crayon, Gent." This quiet stroller and deft sketcher of life about him, this interested but self-effacing spectator who could mix philosophy with amusing leg-pulling, and who had polished talents as a storyteller was, notice, still a "gentleman." As a pioneering American artist Irving felt himself out on a limb, but he was not about to saw away behind if he could help it. Suppose *The Sketch Book* failed?

Of course it did not, for all of what he sometimes disarmingly called his "weathercock" gifts. And here the luck comes in. The first Yankee installments of his work, which included "Rip Van Winkle," were read and praised in London, and were thus in danger of piracy, an occupational hazard for authors then, in the absence of international copyright protection. As Irving recalled it in the "Preface" in 1848 to his "Author's Revised Edition":

> The first volume of The Sketch Book was put to press in London as I had resolved, at my own risk, by a bookseller unknown to fame, and without any of the usual arts by which a work is trumpeted into notice. Still some at-

tention had been called to it by the extracts which had previously appeared in the *Literary Gazette,* and by the kind word spoken by the editor of that periodical, and it was getting into fair circulation when my worthy bookseller failed before the first month was over, and sale was interrupted.

At this juncture Scott arrived in London, I called to him for help, as I was sticking in the mire, and, more propitious than Hercules, he put his own shoulder to the wheel. Through his favorable representations Murray was quickly induced to undertake the future publication of the work he had previously declined. A further edition of the first volume was struck off and the second volume was put to press, and from that time Murray became my publisher. . . .

This rescue operation took teamwork from the most famous novelist of the day (Walter Scott, a recent Irving acquaintance) and the most famous publisher (curmudgeon John Murray II)—a conjunction of planets! But from there on there was no stopping *The Sketch Book.*

The book itself, with somewhat differing United States and United Kingdom elements never then combined, was at first actually two *Sketch Books,* depending on where you bought it. In fullest form it became a miscellany of some thirty essays, sketches, and tales. As Henry A. Pochmann and Gay Wilson Allen put it:

> About half the pieces are based on observations of English life and customs, towns, estates, and places rich in legendary lore and tradition. Six are roughly classifiable as literary essays, four are in the nature of travelling reminiscences. Three others —"Rip Van Winkle," "The Legend of Sleepy Hollow," and "The Spectre Bridegroom"—are short stories. Two deal with the American Indian. The remaining three are so miscellaneous as to defy classification.[3]

If this suggests the table of contents was but a roll of the dice for the author, be assured he was more cautious

7

than that. In most of the "Parts" close examination reveals a pattern in which deliberate effort was made to put together at least three types—a comic piece, a more or less sober or reflective one, and one with a tug at the heart. Not that Irving was just a literary carpenter, any more than Edgar Allan Poe would be, but both had an instinctive sense of the taste of the times. Their muses, however truly inspired, knew something of marketing as well.

When Irving put his final touches to *The Sketch Book* in 1848, he gave to posterity the volume most of us read today. Whatever internal tinkering he engaged in, he retained several lachrymose pieces few now much appreciate, for example, "Rural Funerals" and "The Country Church." But these suited the sensitivities of a Romantic Age that banished skulls and crossed bones from its tombstones and substituted weeping willows. Byron is said to have shed a tear over Irving's melodramatic "The Broken Heart."

More happily, Irving continued to display his evergreen holly wreath of five Christmas papers. These joyous celebrations of ancient Yuletide customs taught early nineteenth-century Americans something about how to "keep" the merry season, even before Dickens and the development of Victorian mores. It is only fair here to add, though, the name of Irving's Knickerbocker acquaintance Dr. Clement Clarke Moore, whose poem "A Visit from St. Nicholas" was first published, unauthorized and anonymously, in 1823. Irving's holiday and holyday "Old Christmas" papers became in themselves perennial favorites, and are still the darling of illustrators and private presses.

His unabashed Englishness, often attacked as anglophilia by chauvinistic countrymen, is one aspect of the fervor of nationalism which Professor Ratner's paper considers. Irving's predilection is clearly (but excusably) reflected in his travelogues "Westminster Abbey" and "Stratford on Avon." Here as a slow-paced guide he took the reader on a tour of two historic shrines with unimpeachable claims to North American reverence. These two

Stratford on avon. Dec 20th 1851

My dear Rodes,

We are thus far on our tour, having visited Oxford Blenheim &c. We shall trace on by "easy stages" visiting the manufacturing towns, & the most important show house on our way, and will be with you on Saturday. (Christmas eve) I am travelling with Mr Van Buren and his son. a young gentleman of about 23 - I hope we shall not crowd your house at this hospitable season, when you must have many of your friends about you - If I find we do, I shall be for releasing you as soon

ILLUS. 3

Stratford on avon Dec. 20th 1831.

My dear Rodes:

 We are thus far on our tour, having visited Oxford, Blenheim &c. we shall travel on by "easy stages" visiting the manufacturing towns, & the most important show houses on our way, and will be with you on Saturday, (Christmas eve) I am travelling with Mr. Van Buren and his son, a young gentleman of about 23. I hope we shall not crowd your house at this hospitable season, when you must have many of your friends about you. If I find we do, I shall be for relieving you as soon as possible, and pursuing our tour.

 With kindest remembrances to Mrs. Rodes

Yours ever

WASHINGTON IRVING.

P.S. We mean to take Newstead Abbey in our line of March and see the improvements made by the worthy Colonel.

Transcript of ILLUS. 3

pieces were so widely influential that even in 1905 Brander Matthews could write, "No single work has been more potent than the 'Sketch Book' in directing to Stratford-on-Avon and through Westminster Abbey the unending procession of transatlantic travellers from America." And this before the jumbo jet!

By contrast, and beyond cavil, the best of his *Sketch Book* materials, and his American materials as well, are the two tales "Rip Van Winkle" and "The Legend of Sleepy Hollow." Carefully constructed and colorfully narrated, they made a classic start for our native short story. It probably matters little, except to the researcher, that for both stories Irving used as sources German folklore and literature. No need for his old friend "Gentle Reader" to trouble much over this because, readymade plots notwithstanding, both stories also contained so much of Irving's genius, especially in adapting Hudson River Valley materials to his purpose for characterization and setting, that they are native triumphs as storytelling.

In "Rip Van Winkle" the author fashioned, from nostalgic daydreaming and legendry both native and foreign, a spectacular success as escapism. His scapegrace hero, complete with the traditional shrewish wife, offers a vicarious flight into carefree irresponsibility. Irving's comic purpose is unmistakable, especially with the introduction of a little "Kaatskill" bowling team, but more serious implications lie as symbolism in his instinctive handling of Nature, especially seen in landscape, as beneficent and restful. Rip himself is virtually immortal, a prime figure in American folklore, still alive as Lewis Leary has said "on stage, on screen, and in the hearts of his countrymen."[4] Rip's most famous reappearance in other media was undoubtedly Joseph Jefferson's nineteenth-century characterization of Rip, a personal tour de force that charmed audiences for half a century.

"The Legend of Sleepy Hollow" is almost as renowned, though a distinction between the two tales is like the proverbial choice between an apple and an orange. Again the Dutch in the Hudson River Valley contributed hugely to a rollicking Irving tale. The very title has given astonishing currency to "Sleepy Hollow" as an idea and an idiom. Ichabod Crane is almost instantly recognizable to most Americans as a figure of fun. Modern scholarship, best voiced by critic Daniel Hoffman, tends to see meaning-in-depth in his plight, wherein "the yokel gets the best of the city slicker."[5] This story too has been a favorite of dramatizers and illustrators; and it inspired an operetta *The Headless Horseman* in 1936, with libretto by Stephen Vincent Benét and music by Douglas Moore.

In a memorial address after Irving's death William Cullen Bryant described the two as "among the most delightful and popular tales ever written." He added, "In our country they have been read, I believe, by nearly everybody who can read at all." A century and a half later, and across the English-speaking world, it is a good guess that this statement is probably still true.

There is no space here to reflect on the years immediately following *The Sketch Book,* except to note that Irving was now a literary lion, even in Great Britain. Through the period of *Bracebridge Hall* (1822), a good book but certainly unspectacular, and *Tales of a Traveller* (1824), which should have been much better, Irving remained abroad, often in Germany or France. At home James Fenimore Cooper was beginning his novels, including *The Leatherstocking Tales,* and with them American literature achieved another whole dimension. Add in William Cullen Bryant's poems and literary criticism, and our profession of letters was having a belated but impressive start.

Castles in Spain had fascinated Irving since boyhood, when his reading had included *Don Quixote.* He could little have guessed, however, when he reached Madrid in 1826, how large for the rest of his life things Hispanic would loom for both the writer and the person. My own paper in this symposium gives details; here I shall note only that, three years later when he left Granada for good, he had labored in this Iberian vineyard as biographer, historian, and Crayonesque sketcher again. The results were mainly three: *The Life and Voyages of Christopher Columbus* (1828), superseded now but then applauded as a "first" in English; *The Conquest of Granada* (1829), which loosely chronicled heroic centuries of Christian versus Moor; and *The Alhambra* (1832), which it may be argued is his greatest success after *The Sketch Book*.

In early 1830 Irving was ensconced in London as Secretary to our Legation. The appointment had been engineered by family and interested friends, yet accolade that it was this proved a working post not just a ceremonial one. Nor is it window-dressing to add that during these final expatriate years the Royal Society of Literature awarded him its Gold Medal in 1830, and the next year Oxford University bestowed a Doctor of Civil Laws. No American man of letters, or diplomat either, had previously received this double honor. The Washington Irving who returned to the United States in mid-1832, after seventeen years, had become his country's boast, judging by a famous testimonial dinner in New York City, and honorary doctorates from Columbia and Harvard universities.

About this time Irving, now into middle age, apparently gave up the ingrained habit of daily journalizing. He had by then filled a score or more of diaries, and as many commonplace books in part, with daily entries recording his life on two continents and almost a dozen countries. Anyone who has ever tried the discipline of such regular jottings can appreciate the task he set himself from youth. In the end Irving accumulated a bookshelf of such personal papers, now widely scattered and some regrettably missing. The journals have already begun to appear, with the literary works too, uniformly edited for the first time, in the definitive *Complete Works of Washington Irving,* supervised by the Modern Language Association's Center For Editions Of American Authors, and published by the Wisconsin University Press. Professor Springer's paper on *The Sketch Book* is informative about the scrupulous editorial techniques involved.

As the other side of his autobiographical coin, Irving wrote a great amount of correspondence. Throughout his life he put pen to paper many thousands of times with family or friends, recent companions, or total strangers. The range and variety of these letters is unusual, as Professor Kleinfield's paper brings out, and the number of these surviving, in private hands or government records or institutional collections, is equally so. Not all writers of his literary age have been so well served by time and human hands. We might wish that Irving's letters revealed more, especially of his creative life. Nevertheless, when published in the Irving Edition these missives, whether fat letter-journals from a distant land, shrewd business mail, or skimpy social notes at home, overall will help describe a remarkable American life and a surprisingly adventuresome career.

One adventure which the Symposium could not cope with, for reasons of time, was Irving's experience with the Far West. His own rediscovery of America began in the summer of 1832, and in the frequently unpredictable fashion of his long history as a hardy traveler, he soon found himself in St. Louis, after the kind of steamboat misadventures Mark Twain would come to celebrate. By now attached to a government expedition to scrutinize unmapped Indian country beyond the Arkansas Territory, the author would journey during October and early November far beyond Fort Gibson into the "Pawnee Hunting Grounds," lands that would not become part of the Oklahoma Territory until 1890.

In his schooldays "West" had meant the Northwest Territory as in the Ohio Valley, or the "Old West" of the Appalachian frontier in Kentucky or Tennessee. Now, with Andrew Jackson in the White House, the first President to grow to manhood beyond the mountains, the spirit of Manifest Destiny was in the air. "West" had become "Far West," a vastness rolling for countless leagues beyond the mid-continent rivers and southward toward the disputed Rio Grande. In the whole of Irving's lifetime no other American man of letters of any consequence had a firsthand experience that could match his own in reaching what came to be called "Indiahoma."

One could wish the literary results were more impressive, but the opportunities here for a practiced and popular writer to rise to the occasion of an extraordinarily different and exceptionally American kind of inspiration and topic were fumbled. It may be that Irving was just too set in his ways and this eye-opening odyssey came too late. But also, as Professor Hedges emphasizes in his contribution, the American in Irving could be ambivalent, with resulting detriment to his native art. Whatever the reasons, in 1835 "A Tour on the Prairies," Part I of *The Crayon Miscellany,* proved too slight and too romantic a reporting of the facts. Irving had indeed crossed the Arkansas River in a raft of buffalo hide, steered by two half-breed guides, and then at once sat down on the west bank to make notes. But his published account missed the excitement of the ride—there was too much East in his West.

In fairness, though, it must be added that because of the actual frontiering he did, Irving was better equipped to handle the genuine fur trade histories that followed, *Astoria* in 1836 and *The Adventures of Captain Bonneville* in 1837. Both, if only for a few seasons, after which they were victims of the onward sweep of history, opened windows on the Rocky Mountain West that gave stay-at-homes a clearer view of transcontinental exploration and our huge natural resources, when these were incompletely known. The mid-twentieth-century passion for Western Americana has helped blow the dust from these neglected narratives.

By the early 1840s Irving, now the proud Squire of his beloved Sunnyside, as Mr. Butler's paper reveals, seemed easing into retirement. A new generation of writers was beginning to assert itself, including Hawthorne and Longfellow, whose early works were indebted to him. When in 1842 President Tyler appointed Irving our Minister to the troubled Spain of Queen Isabella II, seemingly to the new diplomat's surprise, public approval of this proconsular dignity was widespread. For the next four years The Honorable Mr. Irving did full justice to his country's affairs in a Spain which welcomed him back, and in which he remains a clear memory.

On returning to America, edging into his sixties, he could well have settled for comfortable sunset years as a veritable national institution. Professor Gibson's paper samples contemporary opinions of Irving's worth, including some in conflict even at this point. Instead, with the encouragement of George P. Putnam, the rising New York City Publisher who would be his economic mainstay in late years, Irving undertook an entire "Author's Revised Edition" of his now multiplied works. This project, which lasted from 1848 to 1851, resulted in the publication of uniform volumes, and was the first successful venture of its type in our publishing history. This final version, in time illustrated in part by the gifted Felix O. C. Darley, was the usual form except for textbooks in which Washington Irving was read through the late nineteenth and early twentieth centuries.

The final decade of Irving's life, before his death on November 28, 1859, was more ambitious and energetic than might be expected from one who had passed his allotted three score and ten. American literature was now in the vigorous hands of the giants of our "American Renaissance," like Emerson, Thoreau, Melville, and Whitman. Nonetheless Irving retained his special niche in the mid-century Hall of Fame, and his Sunnyside home became a place of literary pilgrimage.

Civic duty occupied his time, as in conscientious service as Chairman of the Board of Trustees of the newly opened Astor Library, a public institution and one parent of the present New York Public Library on Fifth Avenue and 42nd Street. But to the end authorship was his goal. A five-volume *Life of George Washington* (1855-1859), its bright purpose shadowed by the slowness of his pen in

New York April 10th 1842

My dear Sir,

I had intended to call on you previous to my departure, but have been so much hurried as not to find a moment of leisure. I am occupied upon a life of Washington, which I shall finish while in Spain. You must be rich in personal recollections of him, and may have interesting documents concerning him and concerning the American revolution. Any thing of the kind that you can furnish me will be considered a most valuable favor. Should you find it convenient to attend to this application and any letter you may wish to forward to me can be sent to the counting house of Messrs Grinnell Minturn & Co.

With best wishes for your health & happiness

I remain my dear Sir

Yours very faithfully

Washington Irving

Genl Morgan Lewis
&c &c &c

ILLUS. 4

New York April 10th 1842

My dear Sir,

*I had intended to call on you previous to my depart-
ure, but have been so much harried as not to find a moment of leisure. I am occupied upon a life of Washington,
which I shall finish while in Spain. You must be rich in
personal recollections of him, and may have interesting
documents concerning him and concerning the American
Revolution. Any thing of the kind that you can furnish
me will be considered a most valuable favor. Should you
find it convenient to attend to this application any letter
you may wish to forward to me can be sent to the counting house of Messrs. Grinnell Minturn & Co.*

With best wishes for your health & happiness

I remain my dear Sir

Yours very faithfully

WASHINGTON IRVING

Genl. Morgan Lewis

Transcript of ILLUS. 4

ailing old age, closed out a career that spanned nearly sixty years. His nephew and official biographer, Pierre Munro Irving, keeping a notebook over the last days, at one point wrote down this observation by his beloved uncle: "In life, they judge a writer by his last production; after his death, by what he has done best." Washington Irving must have known then, as we do a century and a half later, that his best was *The Sketch Book*.

Notes

[1] Henry Adams, *History of the United States* (New York: Charles Scribner's Sons, 1889), Vol. 1, p. 23.

[2] Van Wyck Brooks, *The World of Washington Irving* (New York: E. P. Dutton & Company, 1944), p. 25.

[3] Henry A. Pochmann and Gay Wilson Allen, eds., *Introduction to Masters of American Literature* (Carbondale, Ill.: Southern Illinois University Press, 1969), p. 49.

[4] Lewis Leary, *Washington Irving* (Minneapolis: University of Minnesota Press, University of Minnesota Pamphlets on American Writers, No. 25, 1963), p. 26.

[5] Daniel G. Hoffman, "Irving's Use of American Folklore in 'The Legend of Sleepy Hollow,'" *PMLA,* Vol. LXVIII, No. 3 (June 1953), p. 433.

Rip Van Winkle.

a posthumous writing of Diedrich Knickerbocker

By Woden, God of Saxons,
From whence comes wensday. that is Wodensday,
Truth is a thing that ever I will keep
Unto thylke day in which I creep into
My sepulchre ——
                                    Cartwright.

Whoever has made a voyage up the
Hudson must remember the
Kaatskill mountains. They are a dis-
membered branch of the great appalachian family, and are seen away to the
west of the river swelling up to a noble
height and lording it over the surrounding country. Every change of season
every change of weather, indeed every hour
of the day, produces some change in the
magical hues and shapes of these mountains, and they are regarded by all the

ILLUS. 5

The Sketch Book

Haskell S. Springer

DURING 1819 and 1820 *The Sketch Book of Geoffrey Crayon, Gent.* was published in seven installments in the United States and in two volumes in England. These same two years saw the birth of George Eliot, John Ruskin, James Russell Lowell, Walt Whitman, and Herman Melville. They also saw the appearance of Shelley's *Prometheus Unbound* and *The Cenci*, the first two cantos of *Don Juan*, Scott's *Ivanhoe*, and Keats' great odes. I mention these other literary events not just to point out a chronological coincidence, but to suggest that *The Sketch Book* does not shame its company. There was no doubt by the foremost British authors of the time, Byron, Coleridge, and Scott among them, as well as by Americans such as James Fenimore Cooper, Nathaniel Hawthorne, and Henry Wadsworth Longfellow, that *The Sketch Book* was art of a high order; and the reading public signified *its* pleasure by buying up every available copy.

The Sketch Book was not only an immediate best seller, but the progenitor of a long line of "sketch books." Volumes entitled "Sketches of this or of that," "Sketches from the pencil of Smith or Jones," and so forth, proliferated in the years following Irving's great success, as inconsequential writers tried to cash in on the market.

One of the reasons for Irving's success is that *The Sketch Book* is, as Huckleberry Finn said in another context, "various." It is a literary potpourri, specifically diversified to appeal to a variety of taste. Therefore, as we read the separate sketches, we find a deliberate shift from mode to mode, tone to tone. But in subject matter, interestingly enough, one broad area predominates. This first internationally renowned American book, by the first successful professional American author, largely focuses on England. Only four of the thirty sketches originally published contain specifically American materials.

Competent literary critics have carefully examined this anglophilic quality, as well as the book's strong sense of mutability, its particular brand of Romanticism, the character of Geoffrey Crayon who is the central persona, the achievement of particular tales and sketches; and rather than repeat what others have said on *The Sketch Book* as literature, I would like instead to talk about *The Sketch Book* as a physical document.

As you know, in dozens of colleges and universities around the country right now, hundreds of scholars are engaged in editing or re-editing the works of our major American authors. You no doubt know too that this editorial work, largely conducted under the auspices of the

Modern Language Association's Center For Editions Of American Authors, formerly headed by William Gibson, has come under attack by no less a literary light than Edmund Wilson, that it is every year attacked anew by the New University Conference, and that it is considered ill-advised by a number of our colleagues, perhaps even some of you here today. With this current state of affairs in mind I would like to speak as nontechnically as I can, from my experience to date in editing *The Sketch Book;* first, to illustrate some important contingencies of authorship in the early nineteenth century; and second, to try to demonstrate to the educated reader the importance of this work for Washington Irving's *Sketch Book.*

Irving had been in England for five apparently unproductive years when, in March 1819, he sent to his brother Ebenezer, in New York, a parcel of manuscript for "the first number of a work to be continued occasionally should this specimen meet with sufficient success." This first installment of five essays and narratives, published in June 1819 (improbably enough by a man named Van Winkle) turned out to be a remarkable commercial success, and so did the succeeding installments. Their fame spread so rapidly that in three months a British journal had already reprinted one of the sketches. Irving became worried that all of the work printed in the United States would appear, unauthorized, from a British publisher. Not only didn't he want an error-filled *Sketch Book* on the market, but he was operating in the absence of an international copyright law and consequently wanted to establish British copyright by publishing *The Sketch Book* in England *himself* before anyone else had the chance, so he arranged with John Miller, a very small London publisher, to put out, at Irving's expense, a volume containing *Sketch Book* numbers 1-4. It appeared in February 1820, but within two months Miller had gone bankrupt. Fortunately, through the influence of Sir Walter Scott, John Murray II (the publisher of Jane Austen's novels, Byron's poems, and the *Quarterly Review*) took over publication on terms favorable to Irving. He first took the remaining unbound sheets of the Miller volume, gave them a new title page reading "second edition," and sold them under his imprint. Then Murray published Volume II, which contained all the material appearing in America as *Sketch Book* numbers 5-7—and more. At this point, still in 1820, there existed two *Sketch Books*: the American version had twenty-eight sketches; the British version contained all these, plus a new headnote and endnote, and two Indian sketches, "Philip of Pokanoket," and "Traits of Indian Character," which Irving had originally published in the *Analectic Magazine* six years before. Some of its sketches were revised, one very heavily. In other characteristics, too, the British and American *Sketch Books* differed according to the quirks of their respective printers.

Second editions soon appeared in both countries, with even more widely differing texts because of certain changes Irving had ordered in the American version. By 1830, at least fifteen more editions had appeared in England and America, some of them dependent on one version, some on the other.

Meanwhile Irving was putting out an English-language Paris edition in 1823, containing further corrections and revisions; and in the same year a slightly altered, authorized *Sketch Book* appeared, in English, in Dresden. Here the *Sketch Book* rested, as far as Irving was personally concerned, for twenty years, though reprints and translations multiplied at a furious rate in a number of countries.

Then, in 1848, Irving published the last edition of *The Sketch Book* in which he personally had a hand. He had contracted with G. P. Putnam for a complete edition of his works, entitled the "Author's Revised Edition." For this edition of *The Sketch Book* he made a number of further stylistic revisions, and then added two complete essays, a postscript to "Rip Van Winkle," a long preface, and assorted notes. From all we can gather, Irving regarded this edition as the final, authorized one, and up to the present, if you buy a paperback copy of *The Sketch*

Book, it will be basically the Author's Revised Edition.

Now where does all this leave you and me, the modern readers of *The Sketch Book?* It leaves us with a book that is not spelled as Irving spelled it, or punctuated as he punctuated it, or even worded as he worded it; a book so controlled by influences and hands other than the author's that at points in the text it seems almost as though Washington Irving were merely a coauthor in collaboration with a composite colleague made up of publishers, printers, compositors, and proofreaders, who have had a distressing combined effect on the book Irving wrote. Let's return to the beginning of the story and look at some major items in the process of "de-Irvingization."

When Irving, still in England, saw a copy of the first printed number of *The Sketch Book,* he wrote back to New York, saying "I would observe that the work appears to be a little too highly pointed. . . . High pointing is apt to injure the fluency of the style if the reader attends to all the stops." Characteristically, Irving's comment was mild and unaccusing; he could justifiably have been irate. Comparing the surviving manuscript (less than half of the whole) with the first three printed installments of the American edition, we find the American printer added about 1,000 commas and semicolons. Obviously that much additional punctuation in about 250 pages was bound to make the work more choppy, much less smooth.

Irving had not been in the States to read proof for that edition, but he did personally oversee the printing of the first British edition. From what text, though, did the British compositors set their type? Why, from the same American edition with all its excessive punctuation. Irving did not have the time or energy to try to restore the rhythms of his manuscript to the British product. The book had to be published quickly to establish copyright, an overriding consideration for a man who depended on royalties for his livelihood.

Though the printers of the separate editions of *The Sketch Book* generally respected Irving's word-choice, each printing house had its own house style, which dictated the handling of punctuation, usage, spelling, syntax, *and,* though it may sound extraordinary, even paragraphing for the sake of a pretty page. I could give many examples in addition to the heavily excessive punctuation, but I'll mention only two: Point 1: We know from Irving's manuscripts for *The Sketch Book* that he spelled mostly in the British fashion — and British spellings do predominate in all the important editions of *The Sketch Book* until the crucial one, the Author's Revised Edition, when Putnam's house style changed everything to American spellings. As I said before, *The Sketch Book* is a very British book. Washington Irving was an anglophile, and his book deals primarily with British materials. The flavor of the work is therefore best presented in the British spellings Irving himself preferred; yet the book you read today does not have that flavor. Point 2: Irving, who was an inveterate antiquarian, also preferred certain slightly archaic though perfectly acceptable forms of words. For example, he used "shew" instead of "show" in his manuscripts for *The Sketch Book,* but you will only find "show" in your copy.

It may sound as though I'm about to indict all nineteenth-century publishers on charges of grand larceny, for stealing from us portions of our national heritage. But the procedures of the day were considered legitimate even by most authors. Moreover, Irving himself is *also* partly responsible for the corrupted *Sketch Book* we read today. When he was reworking his book for the Author's Revised Edition, the final text, which printing of the book did he have in his hand when he made the marginal notations and other changes for that edition? Which printing of *The Sketch Book* did Irving pass on to the compositor in the print shop who set type for this important revised edition? We might think that he would have chosen one of the editions which he himself had supervised through the press—perhaps John Murray's British edition, or the Paris edition of 1823. But instead, the evidence of one surviving printed page containing his handwritten revisions tells us that he most likely used some mere reprint, probably French, probably printed sometime in the 1830s or 1840s. Of course, such a printing is bound to contain all sorts of errors, especially since its compositors most likely had a very limited knowledge of English. And no author, much less one who at the age of sixty-five was revising an enormous body of prose, could be expected to rectify all the errors and infelicities in the text. Perhaps Irving just couldn't lay his hands on any better edition at the moment, but whatever the reason, his unfortunate choice did put *The Sketch Book* that *he wrote* one small step further from *The Sketch Book* that *we read.*

Now, it is proper to ask what will *The Sketch Book* be like after my editorial work is done? Will it, like Melville's *Billy Budd* ever since 1962, have a new title, and major textual changes which will make the book greatly different from the one we have known? Fortunately, *The Sketch Book* will be, in most respects, the same as before. But it will be spelled largely in the British manner; the punctuation will be looser, less rigidly correct—consequently the style will be easier, more flowing; some of the language will have that archaic flavor Irving preferred, and many words will be changed because they are demonstrably not what Irving intended.

Intention is the key concept in all these matters. As I have tried to show, business considerations, legal matters, accepted practice, and chance, all contributed to making *The Sketch Book* something other than what Irving intended it to be. Though each separate departure is in itself slight, and to some minds perhaps inconsequential, in the aggregate they make a great difference. And since the literary critic often makes vital distinctions on the basis of a single word, it behooves the editor to provide that critic with a thoroughly reliable text. Hopefully when *The Sketch Book* appears it will be, as much as is possible, what Irving himself would have liked it to be. I think we owe one of our finest books at least that much.

ILLUS. 6—*Peter Stuyvesant by William Heath*

The Theme
of Americanism
in Irving's Writings

William L. Hedges

WHEN I agreed to take part in this discussion I thought that my topic was to be the nature of Irving's Americanism. I have written at length of his (to me) rather peculiar or complicated or perhaps confused awareness of himself as an American. But when the program was published, the title proved to be something significantly different, "The Theme of Americanism in Irving's Writings." My first reaction was that it was an impossible title. Americanism seemed to me very much a theme that Irving's work does not have. Here is a criterion according to which we tend immediately to contrast Irving with writers like Michel de Crèvecoeur, or Joel Barlow in *The Columbiad,* or Cooper or Whitman or Henry James or Mark Twain, all of whom, much of the time, are very explicitly asking something like the question: "What does it mean to be an American?"

And even if one thinks of related themes, like freedom, individualism, or self-reliance, Irving contrasts sharply with Emerson, Thoreau, Melville, Hawthorne, Whitman, James, Twain, Dickinson, Frost, Cummings, and any number of American writers who seem more specifically concerned than Irving does with something usually very closely associated with Americanism. It seems to me this is the distinguishing feature. There is very little in Irving that compares with the significance of the environment from which they've come, nothing comparable, for instance, to Faulkner's concern with Southernness, Ralph Ellison's concern with Negroness or Malamud's with Jewishness.

As I thought about it further, however, I realized nonetheless that I might do something with the title, as it stands, making a virtue of necessity and capitalizing on the very scarcity in Irving of the overt, serious, and sympathetic investigation of American character, attitudes, and institutions that we find in so many other standard American authors. We may begin by asking, where, if at all, does Irving take his Americanism seriously? A quick run through his works may be useful. As early as *Salmagundi* (1807-1808) we find him (with his collaborator James Kirke Paulding) making fun of British travelers who come to America and write books full of condescending commentary on American manners and behavior. But if *Salmagundi* is ready up to a certain point to defend America by satire against unfair criticism, it can just as easily turn around and whimsically adopt a foreign point of view (in the guise, for instance, of Mustapha Rub-a-Dub Keli Khan, a captured Tripolitan) as a vehicle for lampooning ludicrous American behavior. The nonsensical humor of the early Irving on the whole precludes the establishment of serious themes. The best way to think about the *Knickerbocker History* (1809), for instance, is as a debunking of, and poking fun at, the exaggerated Americanism typical of many writers (Joel Barlow, for instance) in the first forty or fifty years after the Declaration of Independence.

Nor does Irving's long European phase from 1815 to 1832, when the focus of his work was so much on England, Germany, Spain, Italy, and the European past, reveal any great concern with American themes—at least not on the surface. One is tempted to jump right over it and go on to the final period, which begins with *Columbus* in 1828 (and thus overlaps its predecessor). Here at first glance his work would seem to contain much more of what we are looking for. But in fact I doubt whether the histories and biographies which took so much of his time in the later years come to grips any more fundamentally with the national experience than does his fiction. True, the final period finds him working extensively with American materials and subjects—"A Tour on the Prairies," *Astoria, Adventures of Captain Bonneville* (in the Rocky Mountains), the five-volume biography of Washington. But too often picturesque effects, novelty, and spectacle (the Far West) preclude any depth of exploration. The older, more subdued Irving is satisfied with the tameness of a Washington mediating between the extremes of Jefferson and Hamilton. Or he subsumes what might be seen in terms of its unique Americanness under a more generalized (less concerete and specific) viewpoint — Columbus, for instance, representing for Irving not, as for Joel Barlow, the hope and promise of a new world and a new society but the inevitability of the failure of efforts to establish an earthly paradise.

But there is an obvious example of Irving overtly working with the theme of Americanism that I've overlooked in my cursory survey of his work — "English Writers on

America" — which reminds us that, as he toured Europe in the middle period, he was often quite conscious of himself as an American, offspring of a young provincial society, looking at the monuments (many of them ruins) of an ancient civilization. The early pages of *The Sketch Book* (1819-1820), introducing Geoffrey Crayon, makes this clear. And in that book, in the well-known essay I've just mentioned, Irving becomes what is rare for him — downright chauvinistic. "English Writers on America" is an essay that I've never liked, and that on rereading, I find just as objectionable as ever. But now in the framework of the topic I've been given, it becomes particularly interesting.

Here we have Irving defending America against her detractors, British writers, cautioning the British to put by their prejudices and to remember their kinship with Americans. Here Irving is talking about the significance of America and the values of American experience. And it seems to me that on the whole he sounds quite false. He mouths too many platitudes. It's too easy for him to talk about America as "a country in a singular state of moral and physical development, a country in which one of the greatest political experiments in the history of the world is now performing." It's too easy for him to talk about the basically "sound and wholesome" ingredients of American character, about liberty, progress, and the prosperity, and the nation's "sound moral and religious principles." It doesn't ring quite true, especially when he goes on to say that America, with all of its significance, all of its prosperity, all of its democracy, all of its promise for the future, needn't worry about British criticism. Why, if that were so, did he bother to write the essay? It's too easy to see all through *The Sketch Book* his apprehension, mock it though he sometimes may, that as an American in Europe he risks being put down by people who consider themselves his cultural superiors and who, he half suspects, may actually be so. Thus it is hardly surprising that he goes on, at the end of "English Writers on America," to talk about the need for paying close attention to British models in literature and the arts.

It's a very mixed-up piece, it seems to me, on the one hand, ringing the changes on American freedom, and on the other, talking in a somewhat fearful way about all that Americans have to learn culturally from England. Furthermore, the essay shows Irving's snobbery at its worst, as he talks about the character of the British travelers who come to America. By and large, he says, they are Manchester and Birmingham tradesmen. They are little people in England, but because they're British, they feel they can lord it over the Americans. The one interesting thing in the piece, to me, is his talking about the servility of British travelers, their inferior status in England, when they come to America and are warmly and courteously greeted, they assume that Americans must be inferior. Otherwise, why would they pay Englishmen of such low status so much respect?

The subtlety of this bit of social observation commands attention, but why, if Americans are not to worry about English criticism, should Irving be so compelled to put down most English observers of America as Birmingham and Manchester tradesmen? It's clubbing the British with British standards. It isn't new in Irving either, incidentally. *Salmagundi* had taken great delight in feeling itself superior to the parvenu culture of the traveling British hardware salesman.

Throughout this whole piece, there is no humor whatsoever. Elsewhere in *The Sketch Book,* fortunately, one does find a little humor on the subject of the relation between England and the United States, in "The Author's Account of Himself," for instance, in spite of the fact that here again Crayon does some pompous posing. He has a passage on the glorious beauties of American scenery, for instance, which is absolutely false, sheer rhetoric, I think, and a passage on the storied ruins of Europe, which is simply slick. But then he begins to be a bit humorous, slyly ironic, as he says that he comes to England because he wanted to see what "the great men of the earth" are like. He had seen great men in America, but they, he knew, left something to be desired, because, as philosophers insisted (Europeans like the French naturalist Georges de Buffon and the British Dr. Johnson), "all animals," man included, had "degenerated" in America. How he had longed then, says Crayon with a straight face, to get to Europe "to see that gigantic race from which I am degenerated"!

Here Irving begins to be good. This is the witty, the satirical, the comic Irving. And the point that I am leading up to is that when Irving is trying to use the theme of Americanism, or at least when he is trying to work on it seriously, he's not the real Irving, or he's not the Irving who is worth reading. He can defend his homeland comically, as when he satirizes Tom Moore in *Salmagundi* for insulting America. When he deals comically with Americans who take their own country too seriously, in the *Knickerbocker History,* for instance, he's at his best. But when he gets serious he oversimplifies and betrays himself, saying what he thinks his readers expect, not what he believes or feels. (At one point in the mid-twenties he thought of writing a book of American essays; we can be thankful that he didn't.)

So I'm forced back on the notion that what is important is the kind of Americanism that Irving's work reflects, rather than the explicit theme of Americanism in his work. I don't have time to develop the point, but I shall say very briefly that Irving seems to me to be a very complicated kind of American, an extremely ambivalent, uneasy, uncertain American, in some ways a very lonely American. And I say this is in spite of the poise and self-assurance which may be suggested by the elegance of Sunnyside, in spite of Irving's kindness and affability. Irving, I think, was an American torn between bourgeois and aristocratic attitudes, between romantic and classical attitudes, uncertain of the role and function of the writer in a commercial society. And the conflict of attitudes comes through in his best work, in the character of Geoffrey Crayon, for instance, in *The Sketch Book*. For, in spite of the pretentious rhetoric of "English Writers on America," there are some extremely effective things in *The Sketch Book*. And I think there is cultural significance in the way it suggests the uneasy Amercan coming to Europe, not knowing quite what he should make of British aristocracy, wondering whether it is somehow simply comic or something that an American must take terribly seriously. There is a richness of implication here that we miss if we look only at consciously developed theme.

EDITOR'S NOTE

In the new United States the slow growth of copyright protection for literary property paralleled the career of Washington Irving, and his success illustrates both the strengths and weaknesses of the existing law. During his lifetime the only copyright protection for an American author was under a law passed in 1790 limiting guarantees to citizens only. Overseas, English law was vague about such rights for non-Britons, and only in 1854 was it clearly ruled that only British subjects were protected. The obvious result was habitual transatlantic literary piracy. Against this Irving won early battles for self-protection by the device of virtually simultaneous publication on both sides of the Atlantic, with actual first appearance in London. Later, as an established figure in our growing profession of letters, he several times contributed his name and influence to efforts to improve copyright protections. The present system of international copyright laws post-dates him.

ILLUS. 7—*Sir Walter Scott*

The English
Literary Scene
in the 1820s

Carl H. Woodring

W HEN I listed *The Sketch Book* as an important literary event of 1819 and 1820, in an anthology of
English Romantic prose, in 1961, I did not dream
that I would be here on this Halloween. Indeed in giving
a worn copy of *Knickerbocker* to an Irvingite, Lewis
Leary, I opened it, found a page of notes that I had made
twenty years earlier, and could not remember a single
jotting—or even that I had, in fact, made notes on it.

I should like to begin a little earlier than 1820, just as Irving himself began. When he came to England for a second and more prolonged stay, just after the War of 1812 ended in 1815, he found England in troubled times. There were bad harvests in 1816 and 1817. Famine and the "corn law" of 1815 made life extremely difficult for the poor, and not everybody that Irving met was as placid as the William Roscoe that he writes about in *The Sketch Book*.

In 1819 there were riots, and laws were passed restricting civil liberties. The Prince Regent's estranged wife, Caroline, returned at about this time, with a dogged hope of being crowned queen. Her followers could have taught most of the radicals today a good many tricks about how to conduct oneself in the street, and in court, in a way to make as much difficulty as possible.

The pervasive political acrimony brought a return of satire during the period when Irving lived in England. That kind of acrimonious satire (which had, in fact, been practiced by William Gifford and other followers continuously, anyway) we can see in a number of vigorous works by Byron and Shelley: *The Vision of Judgment, The Masque of Anarchy, Swellfoot the Tyrant*. Social and political acrimony were serious concerns of the writers of the time. Every print shop carried virulent caricatures. Minor works of Keats reflect some of this extreme concern over the tensions and hatred among the classes.

Irving made no acknowledgement at all of the acrimony, of the confusion around him, in *The Sketch Book*. His essay on John Bull is an American view, but its satire is certainly softened, as is almost everything he said in the volume about the English. His John Bull is mostly a very sleepy squire. It is sometimes said among students of English literature that Irving seemed impervious to the Romantic movement swirling about him, but members of the Association here will realize that such a view has to be qualified. His historic allusions are perhaps antiquarian, like one aspect of his friend, Scott, rather than alive with the new historic relativism, which is another aspect of Scott.

Irving wrote of scholars in the British Museum without anything like a description of Charles Lamb, who had searched the Garrick collection of plays for *Specimens of English Dramatic Poets,* several years before Irving first began inspecting writers of the past. Lamb would take his own old books to the British Museum to collate with the museum copy of each. He was a pedant, but he was by no means a musty drudge. Irving seems to have had some ironic sense that he himself belonged among these scholars, that there was something distant and disturbing about being such a figure, but he did not indeed write directly and openly as one of those figures. Lamb was quite willing to explore every aspect of the pedant in him. Irving, it is easy to see, was emulating Addison and Goldsmith. There were editions everywhere of all the British essayists, but Lamb and his fellows in England were leapfrogging the eighteenth century to revive the more fervent spirit of what they called "our old authors," which means all authors down to but not including John Locke. Lamb, with his fellow Romantics, returned to the pre-Enlightenment gusto.

We link sentimental pieces like Irving's "The Widow and Her Son" to the eighteenth-century rise of Methodism, the spray of tender emotions in the second half of the eighteenth century. That link is real, but the sentimental humanitarianism of this and of other pieces in *The Sketch Book* connects also with the beginnings at least of the English Romantics Coleridge, Wordsworth, and Southey. Wordsworth called one poem of this type, "Guilt and Sorrow." But the emphasis on such pieces in Wordsworth and in Irving is on sorrow without guilt.

The Excursion, which had been published in 1814, begins with a kindred piece of this kind, which had earlier been called "The Ruined Cottage," just now being touted as one of Wordsworth's greatest poems. Francis Jeffrey, who shared a number of premises with Irving, opened his review with the words, "This will never do."

Irving's best tales in *The Sketch Book* were adapted from the German. Scott, who befriended Irving in various ways, did him the favor of sending him to spectral bridegrooms, demon lovers, pumpkin-headed ghosts, and similar Germanic frolics. *Blackwood's Edinburgh Magazine,* founded in 1817, specialized in these Teutonic things.

Scott himself, like Coleridge, had been translating German for readers of the entire century. But, of course, Irving and Scott liked the Germanic supernatural because of a kinship with the English tradition, which had been revived with Bishop Percy's *Reliques of Early English Poetry,* a tradition spread through many things that were certainly thought of as completely English. It is not German specters that we find in ballads and tales by Keats —and Keats was looking, at least chronologically, on exactly the same England that Irving looked on.

Hazlitt, in *The Spirit of the Age,* complains of Irving's retrogression to eighteenth-century types. He does not mean types of essay, so much as human beings considered as types. A person was considered as a bundle of generic qualities observed through a theory of general nature. And here, Irving does differ from romantic attention to particulars, to the individualizing. His attempts at macabre comedy resemble one of Wordsworth's attempts, especially in the similarity of their comic diction, but Irving differs from Wordsworth, Lamb, Hazlitt, and even Leigh Hunt, because he declines to exploit the egoistic mode. His style, often urbane, never reveals the self within, the self struggling through an inner division into growth. Geoffrey Crayon never makes himself more interesting than his subjects.

Why, if he seemed to Hazlitt and other reviewers of the day an echo of the eighteenth century, did he attract so much attention? Why was he received so warmly by English readers? One reason would be that this became an age of prose, that Percy Shelley's poetry gave way to his widow's novels. But I think—and facts are of no value here—that Irving was accepted throughout England, even by the reviewers who found him a part of the past, because *The Sketch Book* found its audience when the political acrimony of the previous decade began to fade. His essays ushered in the tolerance, the social reconciliations, of the 1820's. *The Sketch Book* pointed the way, beyond romantic energy to what Aleric Watts called "sentiment purified by taste." *The Sketch Book* bridged, in England, the eighteenth century to the Victorians.

EDITOR'S NOTE

When, as Andrew Jackson's Secretary of State, Martin Van Buren (1782-1862) on February 10, 1830 signed Washington Irving's appointment as Secretary to our London legation, he could not have foreseen that he would himself, the next year, arrive in Great Britain as our Ambassador-designate. It was then the two New Yorkers met for the first time. What followed was a decade of friendship that began in warm regard, continued through years of intimate correspondence, and included travel and visits together on both sides of the Atlantic.

The high point was reached in 1838, two years after Van Buren's election as the eighth President, when he offered Irving a Cabinet post as Secretary of the Navy. The author respectfully declined this honor, citing an instinctive distaste for the pressures forced on a man in high public office. Their friendship survived this but soon cooled during the presidential campaign of 1840 when Irving, uneasy with Democratic fiscal policies in particular, supported Van Buren's successful opponent, the Whig candidate William Henry Harrison.

Andrew Jackson, President of the United States of America,

To Washington Irving, Greeting:

Reposing special trust and confidence in your Integrity, Prudence and Ability, I have nominated and by and with the advice and Consent of the Senate, to appoint you the said Washington Irving, Secretary of the Legation of the United States of America, near his Britannic Majesty; authorizing you hereby to do and perform all such matters and things as to the place or Office doth appertain, or as may be duly given you in charge hereafter, and the same to Hold and exercise during the pleasure of the President of the United States for the time being.

In Testimony whereof, I have caused these Letters to be made patent, and the Seal of the United States to be hereunto fixed. Given under my hand at the City of Washington the tenth day of February A.D. 1830; and of the Independence of the United States of America, the fifty fourth.

Andrew Jackson

By the President,

M Van Buren
                                        Secretary of State.

American Nationalism Fifty Years After The Revolution

Lorman A. Ratner

ONE of the rules that I guess we're all taught is that when you are lecturing it's a sin to start out by apologizing. I'm going to sin, and as long as I'm doing it, I'm going to sin twice. The first sin is to say that unlike my colleagues on this panel, I'm not an Irving scholar. I don't pretend to know too much about Washington Irving beyond a layman's and an historian's (and I guess they go together in this panel) kind of knowledge of him, but I am very interested in Irving and a number of other writers of this period, because of the way in which they can help me understand American society, particularly certain aspects of it in the 1820s and 1830s.

So my first sin is that I will not be talking to you very much about Irving, although this is clearly a panel devoted to him. I will try to suggest to you how Irving fits into the pattern that I'll be setting forth.

My second sin is this: I have a very broad thesis to suggest to you, much too broad to try to really do much with in the time available. So I think it best to set down for you a very general idea about American culture in the 1820s and 1830s, an idea that I hope can be pursued elsewhere by my colleagues who know more about Irving than I, in terms of whether Irving fits the pattern that I think we can use him for.

So with that as a rather long-winded preface on what I have to say—my topic is set down as "American Nationalism Fifty Years After The Revolution." Now, the fifty years taken in a figurative way, and intended as figurative, has for me some broad significance. I think there's a theme here and it goes something like this.

Recent historians who have studied the "Age of Jackson" have argued most persuasively that conservatism best describes the dominant political and social attitudes of that age. These historians point to the Jacksonians' frequent allusions to a golden past during which Americans believed a "republic of virtue" had been shaped. Put most simply, the thesis is that in an age of rapid economic growth and geographic mobility, Americans self-consciously sought to stabilize their world, to provide an emotional, intellectual security as a counterbalance to the whirling changes so apparent at the time.

Indeed, it has been suggested that in societies which emerge as a result of some dramatic event, for example, a revolution or a mass migration, fifty years later the people of the society often experience a form of identity crisis. Presumably the logical explanation for this pattern of behavior is that in a half century most of a society's leaders have died. The direct contact with the men who made the new society is gone, and there is fear that with them died the spirit and the intent of the original founders. It was in the 1680s that the New England Puritan clergy most often delivered their jeremiads, sermons warning of imminent doom, and when the response to supposed witchcraft was most extreme. Some observers have suggested that Soviet society is experiencing the effects of losing its last revolutionary participants and that appeals for rededication to the revolutionary spirit and principles have become apparent. While in no way claiming this fifty-year syndrome is a proven thesis, it does provide an interesting point of departure when examining American society fifty years after its revolution from England.

In 1826, as they celebrated the fiftieth anniversary of the signing of the Declaration of Independence, Americans simultaneously were shocked, frightened, and encouraged by the death on July 4 of that year of both Thomas Jefferson and John Adams. They assumed that the dual death on such a significant date must be a symbol, but they were uncertain as to its meaning. It could suggest a final loss of the spirit of the republic or it could mean that God was reminding Americans of the special quality of their society. In either case Americans related the deaths to their concern that the original values, attitudes, and beliefs of their society were in some way in danger of being changed or already had changed.

During the decade of the 1820s dozens of fictional works, novels, plays, and poems, and some biographies, were published in which the authors described and idealized the men who made the Revolution. Well-known leaders and common people emerged as selfless heroes engaged in a noble cause. Before the decade ended the U. S. Congress sponsored a visit to American shores by the aged Lafayette. The idea was to show Lafayette the nation he helped create and presumably to receive his blessing on what in fifty years Americans had wrought. America gave Lafayette a wildly enthusiastic reception, and his polite compliments to his hosts were received as assurance that all was well in the republic. It was people of this society who looked so favorably on the writings of Washington Irving.

As a recounter of legend, a romanticizer of the past, a biographer of Columbus and Washington, Washington Irving produced a literature, even when its setting was European, that appealed to a people who seemed in search of sea anchors to hold against the currents of change so strong in the decades from 1820 to the Civil War. Irving's stories of Dutch New York, England, and Spain may be placed alongside the accounts of faraway places, exotic lands, past times, and foreign worlds, that so often appeared in the newspapers of the 1820s and 1830s. Such literature provided a counterpoint for the mundane world of Jacksonian America. As such it heightened America's sense of national identification.

In thinking of a literature of nationalism too often we assume it must have an American setting and must be chauvinistic. But nationalism also involves the creation of myth and legend. Irving, his friend James Kirke Paulding, and other writers of the day made their contributions to such a body of literature.

Irving, to whatever extent he was the product of such a society and sought to satisfy popular tastes by his success, evidences the extent to which Americans fifty years after the Revolution, sought a national identification and turned to look back at the Revolution and even at their European past to provide that identification.

Andrew Jackson, President
of the United States of America,
To Washington Irving, Greeting:

Reposing special trust and confidence in your Integrity,
Prudence and Ability, I have nominated and by and with
the advice and consent of the Senate, do appoint you the
said Washington Irving, Secretary of the Legation of The
United States of America, near his Britannic Majesty;
authorizing you hereby to do and perform all such matters
and things as to the place or Office doth appertain, or as
may be duly given you in charge hereafter, and the same
to Hold and exercise during the pleasure of the President
of the United States for the time being.

*In Testimony whereof, I have caused these letters
to be made patent, and the Seal of the United
States to be hereunto affixed. Given under my
hand at the City of Washington the tenth day of
February A.D. 1830; and of the Independence of
the United States of America, the fifty fourth.*

Andrew Jackson

By the President,

M. Van Buren

Secretary of State

Transcript of ILLUS. 8

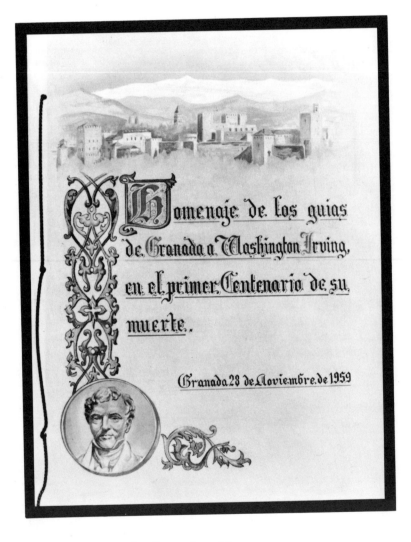

ILLUS. 9—*Tribute by Granada guides*

Irving in Spain

Andrew B. Myers

THERE is a whole book to be written about Irving in Spain; but this afternoon, since we cannot follow him leisurely step by step, I'll do my best to be graceful about a hop, skip, and jump across his years there.

To begin in the present—high on the Alhambra's hill overlooking Granada, in the middle of a little street of shops and homes, opposite the huge and storied palace itself, is the Café-Bar Polinario, a smallish but bustling restaurant with a "two-fork" kitchen and service, long the pleasure of the local *sindicato* of guides. Where the marching legions of the world's tourists, to whom they show this splendid Moorish pile, go to eat is really not the guide's affair; but these well-trained successors to Irving's own Matéo Ximénes regularly repair to a clean, well-lighted upper room of the Polinario to relax and be refreshed. It is, in fact, their private club, and therefore the more significant that the most striking decoration in the room, on the west wall beside the door, is a large marble plaque of Washington Irving. To them, he is the "first" and "father" of all the guides to Granada, a living memory still.

And northward in Madrid, on a very different wall, he is remembered also, and in a manner at least equal to his credit. As one enters the modern block of U.S. Embassy offices at Serrano 75, the left-hand wall of the foyer to the first-floor consulate department has a high marble facade, blazoned at top in brass letters, "Diplomatic Representatives of the United States in Spain." These worthies are listed below, beginning with "Commissioners" in 1777 and continuing through divers changes of names in the nineteenth and twentieth centuries, to the present "Ambassadors Extraordinary and Plenipotentiary."

In mid-nineteenth century the usual style was "Envoy Extraordinary and Minister Plenipotentiary," and proudly counted among these names, for 1842 to 1846, is the name of Washington Irving. His service there, I'm sure, in time made it easier for Thackeray to happen on his compliment to Irving, written shortly after his American friend's death in 1859, that Irving was (I know you've seen this in many a book and heard it from more than one platform) the first "ambassador" from the "New World of Letters" to the "Old."

These plaques are among the fresh honors which symbolize the respect accorded Irving today in a Spain which was long a home-away-from-home for the veteran expatriate. At the same time, one wonders how many of his own countrymen can readily understand in 1970 what

Stanley Williams meant in his authoritative *The Spanish Background of American Literature* (1955), when he wrote of Irving: "No other major writer of the nineteenth century became through residence and use of materials so deeply identified with any one Continental nation."[1] The surest way of comprehending how so Catholic, Latin, and monarchical a culture could come to mean so much to so republican and Protestant a *norteamericano*, may well be to retrace Irving's steps through Spain throughout the years, noting in progress the works from his pen that resulted. However, as I have said, some professorial gymnastics will have to do for the nonce.

To begin with, let's get him to Spain. Irving's first sight of Spain, if not his first steps there, was actually also his first sight of Europe. In late June 1804, when this young unknown of twenty-one was starting on an exciting grand tour, his transatlantic packet first sighted land, on the way to Bordeaux, on the northern Spanish coast—a prophetic landfall we now know!

He actually reached Spain when, at the age of forty-three, and moving down through the Pyrenees with his older brother Pierre as companion, he crossed the border at Irun in February 1826, reaching Madrid four days later. After slightly more than two years there, he left the capital for Andalusia in March 1828. There in the south he would, over the next year or more, travel widely, but also stop for many weeks in Granada and many months in Seville.

In the summer of 1829, now living in the magical Alhambra, Irving was notified of the unexpected diplomatic appointment as Secretary of the U.S. Embassy in London. Duty called, and his unforgettable initial residence in Spain was over. Turning north through Valencia and Barcelona, he eventually recrossed the frontier into France in August 1829, after nearly forty-three months on the Peninsula.

Thirteen years later, now a quite mature fifty-nine, he would in July 1842 return as the U.S. Minister, remaining until July 1846, for a total of forty-eight months of diplomatic service. His life in Spain adds up therefore to some ninety-one months in all, or approximately seven and one-half years.

Today, comparatively few among the general reading public, or even, I think, among students of American literature, to narrow it down to many in the audience, realize fully either the length of Irving's time in this foreign country, or his real intimacy with its culture and people, though they may well know more of the extent of Spanish influence on his literary career.

Popularly as a writer he still means, before anything else, either Dutch New Amsterdam, or the Hudson River Valley, or the Great Britain of song and story. Nevertheless, for half the time he lived in Spain, those initial years in the 1820s, he was a busy professional of letters, though later, while our Minister in the 1840s, his manuscripts were chiefly diplomatic correspondence and letters home. Earlier, however, Spanish influences had powerfully determined the character of three of his more ambitious books: the *Columbus* in 1828, *Granada* in 1829, and the *Alhambra* in 1832. The first two are histories, done in the then-accepted Romantic vein, as in middle years Irving veered from belles lettres to historiography. The artistic value of these works we can speak of later, but now it is enough to say that they have rather faded with time. Ironically, each has a kind of theme of the vanity of human wishes, which even applies to the fate of the books themselves.

The last book, the *Alhambra,* is of course much on the castle itself, but also, in the familiar Irvingesque fashion, about the impressionable author too. Irving's *Alhambra* was, as the American historian William Hickling Prescott (1796-1859) put it, his "beautiful Spanish Sketch-book," one reason why I think it especially appropriate to consider it today, on this anniversary occasion. Indeed, on the title page of the first American edition of the *Alhambra* was put "By The Author Of The Sketch Book." And the title page of the first English edition, also in 1832, included "By Geoffrey Crayon."

The *Alhambra* remains, I feel certain, the most attractive and durable of all his writings on Spain, so we may properly consider it for a time, even at the cost of slighting lesser Spanish pieces like, for example, *Legends of the Conquest of Spain*. Still keeping in mind all his works, all the bits and pieces later put out relating to *España*, one can I think accept the spirit of Stanley Williams's quotation, which follows, though whether he is exactly right in all of his appreciation of individual books must be discussed at another time. Says he,

> Altogether on Spain Irving wrote some three thousand pages and approximately one million words, amounting to about one third of his total writings. Although he is still known as the traditional interpreter in American literature of old England, he devoted far more space and effort to his books on Spain. Nor are these inferior. The *Columbus* and the *Granada* are the equals of *Bracebridge Hall* and *Tales of a Traveler*, and, except for one or two classic tales, such as "Rip Van Winkle" or "The Legend of Sleepy Hollow," they include some of his best writing. Apart from these, the *Alhambra* is the peer of *The Sketch Book*. To understand Irving we must recognize the importance of his writings on Spain.[2]

It is useful also to stress the considerable knowledge he had of that Spain where he is saluted today as *Hispanista,* a tribute not merely to his affection for Spain, his sympathy for things Hispanic, but to his close knowledge of Spain, as well. And I think reference should be made to his knowledge of the language, as well as the people.

He wrote, in one of the family letters alluded to this morning, and referring to his studies of Spanish,

> to those who know French & Italian, (*it*) is a very easy language—The more I am familiarized with the language the more I admire it. There is an energy, a beauty, a melody and richness in it surpassing in their combined

proportions all other languages that I am ac-
quainted with.[3]

And he concluded, "It is characteristic of the nation; for
with all its faults, and in spite of the state into which it
has fallen this is a noble people, naturally full of high
and generous qualities."

The three books already mentioned now get the hop, the
skip, and the jump with apologies to the shade of the
genial if usually unathletic Mr. Irving. First, for reasons
of chronology of course, to *Columbus*. This book, in its
day, was the first effort by an American writing history
to confront the mysteries of Columbus's life and works.
For a time, before more significant books superseded it,
Irving's effort was a matter of genuine reading interest for
a generation of Americans who had nothing exactly to
compare it with. Today, it is all but ignored, significantly
enough, by modern Columbus scholars like Salvador de
Madriaga and Samuel Eliot Morison, but it was much
read in its era, on both sides of the Atlantic, and in its
time received praise even from some Spanish critics, like
the late nineteenth-century Menéndez y Pelayo.

Irving's value in *Columbus* is, I suppose, for the uncrit-
ical reader, and is summed up for our time by Professor
Lewis Leary who writes, "Incidents from Navarettes's
book (*the Spanish scholar from whom Irving culled much
of his information*) were elaborated with bits and pieces
from other chronicles, and the whole was polished until
it shone attractively as a straightforward narrative of
exotic color and maritime adventure."[4]

The *Granada* he himself described in another private
letter, as a "kind of chronicle" in which he had,

> modelled and wrought up the whole into a
> kind of romantic history, in which the chrono-
> logical order of events is faithfully observed
> and every fact is drawn from historical
> sources; having consulted every chronicle,
> private or in manuscript that I could lay my
> hands on. I have endeavoured to throw over
> the whole a colouring that may give it some

thing of the effect of a work of the imagination.[5]

It seems to me Irving might better have stuck in his own person, to history recounted in however "romantic" the fashion of his age, and let the "colouring" go. Except as an equivocal kind of chronicle, as Professor Hedges has shown, the book has not worn well. Still, who could then have guessed the standard of scholarship to be set as quickly as 1837 by the *Ferdinand and Isabella* of Prescott? This classic history, including the conquest of Granada, and with passing praise for Irving's efforts, was done with breadth and depth, though not with discrimination of style, and knocked Irving out of contention for honors. Within a decade it made "Fray Antonio Agapida's" succession of warlike tableaux less the vital reference work than the attractive coffee-table book.

This brings us from the book title to the place—Granada —or, as borrowing from Calderón, Irving wrote in a letter, "Granada, *bellissima* Granada!" The best of Irving's long experience in Spain was Granada, particularly his life there in the Alhambra itself. The book which resulted is still regarded, even in Spain, as the most significant effort made by an American of his generation to know *España* and to interpret her to others.

Irving wrote at one point, "The common people of Spain have an oriental passion for story-telling and are fond of the marvelous." As the first edition of the *Alhambra* would show, on this score its author could meet anyone more than half way. The carefully revised edition of 1851, in which form most readers know the book today, is actually an improvement, as story-telling.

Professor Edward Wagenknecht concluded that the *Alhambra*

> combines *Arabian Nights* material, in the stories told, with honest, straightforward description of the place as it was in Irving's time, and of the people he encountered there. As he himself says, "Everything in the work relating to myself and the actual inhabitants

of the Alhambra is unexaggerated fact; it was only in the legends that I indulged in *romancing.*" As romancing it was very good.[6]

And it was good enough in its factual elements as well to be more than just a clever confection. As far back, or ahead if you like, as 1881, Charles Dudley Warner, in a late Victorian study of his countryman, recognized this combination, "The book abounds in delightful legends, and yet these are all so touched with the author's airy humor that our credulity is never overtaxed; we imbibe all the romantic interest of the place without for a moment losing our hold upon reality. The enchantments of this Moorish paradise become part of our mental possessions without the least shock to our common sense."[7]

But all the pieties of literary history aside, the proof of the *Alhambra* is still in the perusing, and the need to reprint this book, generation after generation, should explain itself.

For reasons of time it is difficult to say anything in detail about Irving's life as a diplomat in the 1840s. It must suffice to say that these years in Spain, which unfortunately had too little to do with his literary interests, found him, for all his merely amateur capabilities as a gentleman of the arts unexpectedly appointed envoy, still well able to handle himself in whatever infighting was necessary to represent American interests in Spain. Indeed, his considerable personal charm made his talents as a socializer a positive advantage.

He came home from Spain in 1846 quite ready to retire, putting away the gold-braided uniform and dress sword that I have seen displayed at Sunnyside.

My title being "Washington Irving *in* Spain" not *"and,"* I must resist the temptation to move through the years with the history of Spain's continuing attention to Irving. But it deserves noting that, for example, just as we are celebrating his *Sketch Book* here, on its 150th anniversary, in 1959, in Granada, on the 100th anniversary of Irving's death, a three-day celebration took place, involving the

University, the city government, and the state office which manages the Alhambra itself. This resulted in speeches, publications, and even in the unveiling of yet another Irving plaque in Granada. All this certainly represents a living memory.

The one thing that keeps that memory most alive is, I think, the presence almost everywhere in Spain of the *Alhambra* itself — the book. It is almost impossible to move about the peninsula without happening on brand-new copies. These are sold everywhere, in English or Spanish versions, to say nothing of French or German or Italian translations, and so on. Hardly a bookshop or newsstand, especially in the railway stations, airports, and hotels of major cities, is without inexpensive paperback editions; and inevitably, in Granada, there are more substantial hardback copies, often brilliantly illustrated with color photographs.

Present too in Granada, at least in the hand of some Americans, younger and older too, are dogeared copies of *Spain on 5 Dollars A Day,* which has its little joke about the summer tourist crowd equipped with copies of Washington Irving's book, which will never be read. Not guilty! How about you, Gentle Reader? Stanley Williams did read it—back to that Hispanophile and Irvingite—who rightly said *Alhambra* was, "besides a garland of distinguished essays, a guidebook for other American Travelers."[8]

In this easy combination of the poetic and the pragmatic our twentieth century can best see the contribution of Irving-cum-Spain to our literature, and to cultural relations between these two highly dramatic civilizations. To most of our contemporaries, reading him in the Western hemisphere, and in English, Washington Irving automatically means "Rip Van Winkle" and "The Legend of Sleepy Hollow" before anything else. It means next, perhaps, nostalgic transatlantic pieces like "Westminster Abbey" and "Stratford on Avon" in *The Sketch Book* too, then possibly the "old Christmas" pages there too. Understandably he is "Geoffrey Crayon" or "Diedrich Knickerbocker" before he is "Don Washington Irving."

But the close student of our cultural history will never underestimate the bonds between Spain and Irving, especially the Irving who could write, in "The Author's Farewell to Granada" at the end of the *Alhambra,* that leaving there ended "one of the pleasantest dreams" of his life. In another sense Irving's dream has never ended, as his fellow countrymen have discovered, with his help, and throughout Spain, in every generation since.

Notes

1 Stanley T. Williams, *The Spanish Background of American Literature* (New Haven, Conn.: Yale University Press, 1955), Vol. II, p. 44.
2 *Ibid.,* p. 38.
3 Stanley T. Williams, ed., *Washington Irving and the Storrows* (Cambridge, Mass.: Harvard University Press, 1933), p. 114.
4 Lewis Leary, *Washington Irving* (Minneapolis: University of Minnesota Press, University of Minnesota Pamphlets on American Writers, No. 25, 1963), p. 33.
5 Williams, ed., *Washington Irving and the Storrows,* p. 134.
6 Edward Wagenknecht, *Washington Irving: Moderation Displayed* (New York: Oxford University Press, 1962), p. 179.
7 Charles D. Warner, *Washington Irving* (Boston and New York: Houghton, Mifflin and Company, 1881), pp. 251-52.
8 Williams, *The Spanish Background of American Literature, op. cit.,* Vol. I, p. 64.

London, May 13th, 1819

My dear Brevoort,

By the ship which brings this I forward a third number of the Sketch Book, and if you have interested yourself in the fate of the preceding I will thank you to extend your kindness to this also. I am extremely anxious to hear from you what you think of the first number — I am looking anxiously for the arrival of the next ship from N. York. My fate hangs on it — for I am now at the end of my fortune. I am writing in excessive haste for the parcel by which this goes is about to be closed.

Give my sincere regards to Mrs. Brevoort and believe me my dear fellow

Ever yours,

WI

The MSS: has gone under care to
Mess. Irving & Smith

Transcript of ILLUS. 10

London, May 15th 1819.

My dear Brevoort,

By the Ship which brings this I
forward a third number of the Sketch Book, and
if you have interested yourself in the fate of the
preceding I will thank you to extend your kindness
to this also.   I am extremely anxious to hear
from you what you think of the first number
& am looking anxiously for the arrival of the
next Ship from N York - My fate hangs on it -
for I am now at the end of my fortune - ~~these~~
the I am writing in excessive haste for the parcel
by which this goes is ~~all~~ about to be closed -

Give my warm regards to Mrs Brevoort
and believe me my dear fellow
ever yours.
WI.

The M.S.S: has gone under cover to
Messs. Irving Smith.

ILLUS. 10

Irving: As Seen
Through His Letters

Herbert L. Kleinfield

I RVING'S letters constantly supply knowledge about
many points that have been discussed here today. In
reference to Cooper, for instance, I have in mind a
letter Irving wrote in 1822, when he was in London, and
Cooper apparently asked him to try to market *The Spy*
among British publishers. Irving explained that although
he admired the book immensely, some pirated edition was
already available. He advised Cooper on how to go about

getting the English copyright in the future before American publication. This shows both that he helped other writers and that they looked to him as an important figure as well as a means to advance their own work.

The question of Irving's Americanism, of course, appeared in his letters constantly, especially in the early years. When *The Sketch Book* first came out, it won him a name; and he repeatedly insisted he had no intention of deserting his native land. He was conscious of being an American and yearned to go home. Homesickness was one of his constant themes, as a matter of fact, but it took him a long time to cure it when he came back seventeen years after his departure in 1815.

But I don't mean to recite to you the contents of the 2,500 Irving letters we have collected for an edition of *The Complete Works of Washington Irving*. I don't know them all. I did read a portion of them for this meeting, particularly those from the period of *The Sketch Book*. We have copies, largely from manuscript, of upwards of 2,500 Irving letters. Dr. Myers and I estimate that these represent approximately half the letters Irving might have written in his lifetime. Five thousand letters seem to me a literary career in themselves, and along with two dozen volumes of published and unpublished work they form an impressive career.

Irving's letters can be divided into four principal types: first, the personal letter, written to his family and close friends; second, a kind of body of literary letters, those concerning his writings and his relations with his publishers; third, social correspondence, consisting of such things as letters of introduction, acceptances and refusals of invitations, and social events; and fourth, his diplomatic correspondence. The letters give us a sense of what kind of person he was. This material is useful to readers, scholars, and people of an inquisitive nature.

Let me explain these divisions a little more fully. Personal letters are clearly the most interesting and they reflect Irving's habits, his relatives, and his activities.

I think the most outstanding single trait they show is his strong family attachment. He had a tremendous sense of loyalty to his relatives, especially to his brothers, all of whom were older, as you know, and to whom he felt immense gratitude. They staked him, first of all, to the tour in Europe in 1804, and helped him out in numerous ways. He tried to do his part to save the failing business in the years between 1816 and 1818, and was deeply involved in the bankruptcy in 1818, in Liverpool. There is a good portion of that attachment and loyalty in these letters. And these are qualities for which we have no other evidence.

We also hear an occasional note of restiveness toward his brothers because he sees them as apparently inflexible and lacking any sense of imagination about his own role. He feels out of step with the business world; he just can't breathe in an office.

Among these personal letters are those he wrote on his various travels. The early tour in 1804 seems to have established a practice in which he wrote a report or guidebook of his travels. He gave his itinerary and observations and descriptions. He did this later as well. When he traveled in Germany in 1822 and 1823, he wrote to his sister Catherine, or to his brother Peter, or to his friend Emily Foster, in the same eminently descriptive way. When he came back to this country and toured the West, before he wrote "A Tour on the Prairies," he wrote long letters to his sister, Catherine Paris. When he returned to Spain he did the same thing and he even wrote more and longer letters to Mrs. Paris' daughter, Sarah, then Sarah Storrow.

Among these personal letters, too, are those of younger adulthood when he addressed his cronies, his good friends, like Henry Brevoort or Charles Robert Leslie, the painter. Here Irving appeared in somewhat different garb than he does through his traveling, because he's witty and gay, genial, exudes bonhommie and camaraderie which is not present in letters to his family. When he writes to his brothers, he is a much more sober gentleman and though he expresses warmth, it is of a different kind.

One more aspect of these letters I might touch on is that they show his friendship with painters. It's rather interesting that Irving had a number of close friends who were eminent painters of their time, including Washington Allston, Charles Robert Leslie, Gilbert Stuart Newton (the nephew of Gilbert Stuart), Sir David Wilkie, and quite a few lesser known people as well.

These friendships reflect Irving's own artistic leaning. He was a sketcher with crayon. He felt, I think, a common ground among creative men and he tended to identify with them. Perhaps this was some kind of hopeful fantasy on his part. He enjoyed painting, he enjoyed visiting museums when he traveled in Germany, Bohemia, and Spain. When he was in Southern France, in 1804 and 1805, he traveled and visited churches where the French Revolutionists still left their mark in destroying statuary and ornamentation. Perhaps he was snobbish and aristocratic about it, but he was offended, I think, because of the injury to art.

Irving had an observant eye, too. I think if there's a single strong trait in his prose, it's his descriptive ability with language; and his response to a painting—if he went to a studio of Leslie or Newton—was to analyze and enjoy it and to express in a letter to one or the other about the third, how he felt this was likely to develop, or what one of these men could accomplish as a painter. So this is, it seems to me, an insight into both his mind and feelings.

The second category, the letters on literary affairs, are not very numerous and some of this material appears in what I am calling personal letters. I see in them a quality of modesty about his own accomplishments. He voiced constant misgivings about his talent and prospect for further success, especially after *The Sketch Book* won him what was genuinely for him an unexpected recognition.

Also, he talked about what he was trying to do or what he felt he has failed to do, giving an insight into the sense of his consciousness that craftmanship was a necessary element of his work. This, I think, is one of the characteristics for which later writers, particularly Longfellow and Hawthorne, regarded him so highly.

These letters in which he talks about his literary work, too, show him aware of his own defects, and they complain in what I think is a rather suspicious way, sometimes, of his inability to write fluently. "To get into the vein" is the phrase he uses over and over again. He was easily distracted from his writing, blocked, you might say, by any number of disturbances. He was often in poor health, particularly in the years of his greatest productivity in the twenties. Perhaps this was an expression of a kind of nervous disorder, functionally speaking. But we can learn more about this from his letters. And he excuses his failure to write, on these various grounds, which might, for people psychoanalytically oriented, be really quite a neon sign, but I don't want to get into these matters now.

There are a few letters, not very many, I regret, to his publishers. The largest number are to John Murray, which some of you may know, have been collected in a volume by one of our Irving editors, Ben Harris McClary, discussing Irving's relation to his publishers. There are a couple of letters to Carey and Lea, the Philadelphia publishers, and to Constable. They speak pretty much in the same vein, a little more formally, about his literary affairs.

There's only one letter, unfortunately, written to George Putnam, and I don't believe it's authentic. I have the same letter six times over. Each of these is a facsimile of an original which I think no longer exists. It may yet turn up, I hope. And curiously enough, this facsimile shows two and a half lines that have been edited out and consist only of dots. The letter thanks Mr. Putnam for sending him a package of books for Christmas, and I just can't quite conceive what might be objectionable that anybody would want to remove from a letter of that kind. For those who want to be very precise, that letter was written on December 27, 1852, and I don't think it's the equivalent of Mark Twain's *1601*.

I know of no other surviving Putnam papers. A member

of the present G. P. Putnam's firm informed me that all the Irving papers and other materials of that archaic character, in which they are no longer interested, were destroyed in a warehouse fire in the 1930s, and that fire may be a symbol.

The third category of letters is his social correspondence. I think, frankly, these are largely trivia. However, put together, these letters give us some instructive thoughts, mostly in the sense of reflecting Irving's very broad acquaintance and large friendship in life, among people of many different walks and stations. He wrote many letters of introduction, six of them in 1827 for the young Longfellow in Europe for instance. He had an active social life, and also he was looked towards for many, many things, particularly when he came back (in 1832) to this country where he received honorary Doctor's degrees from Columbia and also from Harvard. He was nominated to any number of societies, all of which he graciously accepted and explained that he had no intention of appearing.

Irving disliked immensely any public appearance. These social letters show us the conflict he felt over being in the public eye—seeking a kind of seclusion that he felt fitting to his natural modesty and at the same time keeping up a busy social calendar that reflects the popularity and recognition and success that he so eagerly sought.

Fourth, the diplomatic correspondence has practically never been published. It isn't very large, but it is a useful addition to the full picture of Irving's life and work. We see him in contact here with men of distinguished public station — Webster, for instance, John Calhoun, James Buchanan, and when he was Secretary of the London legation in the early thirties, with Louis McLane, who was then the Minister to England and was a rather distinguished diplomat of the day; we also see Irving's contact with Spanish officials. Irving never moved very close to these people, he was not in their circles, except in some distant official capacity, but he did partake of events. He was connected, as Minister to Spain, with American interest in Cuba, and relations that are part of the background that really still stay very closely to us. Moreover, these letters give some more flesh to those personal letters in which he describes his court life to Sarah Storrow, for instance, the pageantry of Spanish receptions which he describes at great length, or to a small collection of letters written to Prince Dimitri Dolgorouki, who was Attaché at the Russian Legation to Spain when Irving was there in the late twenties and became one of Irving's closest friends.

To sum all of this up, I think one may say that Irving grows familiar through his letters in a kind of composite way. We have very little in the way of candid revelations. There are no soliloquies here in which he gives his secret thoughts, although occasionally to Henry Brevoort he wrote more of his loneliness and homesickness in the early 1820s. But put together, the letters are kind of internal evidence and a record of events, of relations, of localities, people in Irving's life, and I think they add up to a man I could try to describe at great length.

Instead I will simply list some of his most prominent characteristics. First, he is a man of serious intentions, however confused or conflicting they may be. He has very conventional—Mr. Hedges called them bourgeois—beliefs, but very strong moral principles and deep attachment to them. He is a man of great sympathy for other people's sufferings. Sometimes he writes about them with an overly saccharine pen, but he himself suffered a number of disappointments and was very sensitive to the troubles of others.

Also, we see a man of considerable self-satisfaction. I don't know that he was ever smug about it, but he had, I think, some genuine sense of pride in what were rather moderate attainments, and I think moderate in the large picture. In his own time, they were perhaps immense. But overall, the letters, I think are most valuable in giving us a sense of Irving as a human being.

ILLUS. 11—*Sunnyside, contemporary drawing*

ILLUS. 11(a)—*Sunnyside, before 1835*

Washington Irving and His Home, Sunnyside

Joseph T. Butler

IN 1798, because of an extensive yellow fever epidemic in Manhattan, Washington Irving at the age of fifteen spent a period of time in Paulding's Manor, close to the present village of Tarrytown. Much later in his life, after extensive periods abroad, he again went to the same area to visit his close friend, James Kirke Paulding (1778-1860). At some point, whether in his youth or on a later visit, Irving saw the old stone house that had originally belonged to Wolfert Ecker, but in the nineteenth century had been acquired by the Van Tassel family. This particular dwelling, a simple tenant farmhouse on a property of twenty-four acres, was originally part of Philipsburg Manor, built in the late seventeenth century.

Irving was deeply interested in the local history of the region. It was perhaps natural that when he wished to escape the urban life of New York City by retiring to the country, he would look to this area because of his fond remembrances of it. So in 1835 he bought the house, which at that particular point was called the Van Tassel farmhouse. Soon after purchasing the house, his friend, the English-born painter George Harvey (c. 1800/01-1878) did a sketch of it revealing a simple regional farm structure of which a number of examples still exist today.

Irving had been exposed to romantic European architecture during his travels abroad. So, with Harvey's aid, he set about remodeling the house to create a unique example of American architecture. No other example in the country is directly comparable, because it is such a highly personal creation. Since, at the time, there were few trained American architects, Irving's ideas were transmitted through Harvey to local builders.

The former small tenant house was actually enlarged in this first stage of architectural change. In 1837, the year that Irving moved into his new home, Harvey produced an engraving of Sunnyside with its stepped gables, weather vanes, and rooms added at the rear. Irving had many relatives and guests staying at Sunnyside with him over the ensuing years. After the first decade of occupancy, during which he used the study as a kind of one-room apartment, he decided to build an addition to the house. In 1848 Felix O. C. Darley (1822-1888), did a drawing of the tower addition built the previous year; at the time it was called "the Pagoda." This tower wing contains servants' rooms on the first floor, and a guest room on the second floor where overflow guests or family stayed. The top floor, used primarily for storage, was a kind of whim,

ILLUS. 11(b)—*Sunnyside in 1836*

ILLUS. 11(c)—*Sunnyside by Currier & Ives*

as it is not possible to see from the windows in any direction because of their high placement.

The house and its additions was publicized throughout this country and, indeed, throughout the world, by a lithograph published by the New York firm of Currier and Ives about 1870. Decades before that Sunnyside became a mecca for people who were interested in literature and the arts, and in conversing with Washington Irving, who always greeted visitors in a most personable way. The print depicts him in the late years of his life sitting on a rustic chair near the driveway to the house.

Irving's study was pictured in Benson Lossing's history *The Hudson, from the Wilderness to the Sea* (1866). The study is probably the most interesting room in the house and one of the best documented rooms in America. The great alcove in the rear contains the divan which he actually used as a bed during the first ten years of residence; the desk was given to him by his publisher, G. P. Putnam. In 1860, the painter Daniel Huntington (1816-1906) sketched several views of the study, which provide excellent documentation for the room. He pictured the arrangement of the room looking toward the south, toward the fireplace wall and carefully depicted Irving's desk and chair. Resting on the mantelpiece in the study are two illustrations by George Cruickshank (1792-1878) for the *Knickerbocker History,* and hanging between them a steel engraving of Sir Joshua Reynolds and his literary circle.

The dining room, which is directly across the hall from the study, often was the scene of Washington Irving's bounteous hospitality. On the west wall hang portraits of the Maryland writer, John Pendleton Kennedy (1795-1870) and his wife Elizabeth, attributed to William J. Hubard (1807-1862). A nineteenth-century visitor who had been at Sunnyside wrote that he had the pleasure of dining in Mr. Irving's dining room with the two Messrs. Kennedy, one at the table and the other hanging on the wall. Also hanging in the dining room are two familiar portraits of Irving. The painting by Charles R. Leslie

(1794-1859) shows Irving when he was about thirty-seven, while the painting by Gilbert Stuart Newton (1794-1835) depicts the author in his forties.

The focal point of the parlor was the piano, as the evening's entertainment often involved music. Irving's nieces, Catherine and Sarah, were talented at the piano while Irving himself played the flute. The piano was made by the New York firm of Nunns, Clark and Company, who worked during the 1830s and 1840s. The sofa was made by two cabinetmakers, Slover and Taylor, who worked in partnership in New York in 1804 and 1805. Nearby is a chair in the "klismos" style of about 1820, which comes from the workshop of Duncan Phyfe. Most of these things were probably brought to Sunnyside from New York.

In 1847, with the completion of the tower, Irving moved into the upstairs bedroom over his study. It is on the east side of the house, away from the noise of the railroad and from the humidity of the river, which suited Irving's needs. The handsome Sheraton bed is an Irving possession which was brought from New York. The balloon-back chairs represent the last style of furniture with which Irving was familiar, the Louis XV Revival Style, which was popular in the 1850s and 1860s.

Irving's nephew, Pierre Munro Irving (1803-1876), occupied a small bedroom close to his uncle as he was deeply involved with Irving's major biographical work, the *Life of Washington*. We are told that this room, at one point, had books that were stacked nearly to the ceiling.

In 1835, Irving wrote that he wanted alcoves at either end of the guest bedroom, and drawings are actually included in the letter. The other end of the room, he instructed, was to be covered with striped paper to simulate the interior of a tent; Irving had seen an "irregular attic room managed in that way in France."

The kitchen is one of the most charming rooms at Sunnyside; late in his life, Irving had a number of improvements installed there. Open hearth cooking had been the manner of the day when he first moved to Sunnyside,

Illus. 11(d)—*Sunnyside, oil by Inness*

but about 1850 Irving installed a cooking range, a copper
heater next to it, and also a rather ingenious method for
piping hot and cold running water in the iron sink on the
other side of the room. The table in the center of the room
is actually a piece of seventeenth-century Hudson River
Valley furniture, which by the 1850s would have been
relegated to the kitchen because of its lack of fashion.

To a great extent it is the landscape setting of the house
which gives it a totality of romanticism. Still to be seen are
the ancient trees and plantings which abound in the paintings by members of the Hudson River School which have
contributed to the fame of the river during the nineteenth
century. Irving referred to Sunnyside as a "snuggery," a
"nook," he even referred to it as a "mansion." But by
whatever name, it is one of the most ingenious and interesting pieces of architcture executed in this country.

ILLUS. 11(e)—*Irving's study*

ILLUS. 11(f)

"Washington Irving and His Literary Friends at Sunnyside," oil on canvas, by Christian Schussele, (1824 or 1826-1879), Philadelphia, 1863. Shown are, left to right: Henry T. Tuckerman, Oliver Wendell Holmes, William Gilmore Simms, Fitz Green Halleck, Nathaniel Hawthorne, Henry Wadsworth Longfellow, Nathaniel Parker Willis, William H. Prescott, Washington Irving, James K. Paulding, Ralph Waldo Emerson, William Cullen Bryant, John Pendleton Kennedy, James Fenimore Cooper and George Bancroft.

BRYANT, WEBSTER, AND IRVING
AT THE MEMORIAL SERVICES FOR JAMES FENIMORE COOPER, FEBRUARY 24, 1852
After a sketch by Dan Huntington.

ILLUS. 12

The American Literary Scene 1815-1860

William M. Gibson

IT occurred to me that it might be more interesting to speak of a kind of spectrum of contemporary reaction to Irving by his contemporaries, from men whom we remember today, rather than talking about Jacksonian Democracy or individualism or transcendentalism or Irving as the father of American literature.

My notion was to speak of the opinions of Cooper, Emerson, Thoreau, Poe, Longfellow, Hawthorne, and Melville, but time will not permit this. Instead, let me give you a sampling of this kind of opinion, starting with the bottom, the bottom being James Fenimore Cooper, and I think the reasons for this are interesting.

At the very opening of Cooper's literary career, Irving was involved in the English publication of *The Spy*, displaying a characteristic generosity. I have a feeling that Irving, in his time, was much like Howells after the Civil War. He was extraordinarily generous in supporting the work of his contemporaries and younger men. But this is what Cooper was writing in May 1833 to the publishers Carey and Lea:

> Your bread and cheese of Mr. Irving is very pretty talking, but I know the man's career too well to admit of any comparison between us. A man who takes the money of the U. States with one hand, and that of the Editor of the Quarterly Review with the other, will never live on bread and cheese, when anything else is to be had.

You can see that Cooper did not care for Irving. Rufus Griswold, the editor, in 1842, tried to reconcile the two men. He'd written that Bryant wondered why Cooper did not understand Irving, who was one of Cooper's very warmest admirers. And Bryant reported through the poet Fitz-Greene Halleck that Irving was very enthusiastic about *The Pathfinder*, that he thought Cooper a man of genius of the first order, a supreme novelist and a fine historian. And he made it his excuse, when writing to Cooper in this fashion, that he admired both men so greatly, that he was a friend of both, that he would like them reconciled.

Cooper responded thus:

> Bryant, however, does not understand *me* instead of my not understanding Irving. My opinion has been independent of what that gentleman might have said of me, or my writings, or character. It has been solely formed on what are admitted to be his acts, and what I think of *them*. I never understood that Irving was severe on me, either as a man or an author; ... A published eulogy of myself from

Irving's pen could not change my opinion of
his career. His course in politics was of a piece
with all the rest, and was precisely what had
been predicted of him, by those who knew
him. Cuvier had the same faults as Irving, and
so had Scott. They were all meannesses, and I
confess I can sooner pardon crimes, if they
are manly errors. I have never had any quar-
rel with Mr. Irving, and give him full credit as
a writer. Still, I believe him to be below the
ordinary level, in moral qualities, instead of
being above them, as he [is] cried up to be.
I believe the same to have been the case with
Scott, whom I knew for a double dealer...
Bryant is worth forty Irvings, in every point
of view, but he runs a little into the seemly
school.

There's a good deal more of this. Let me give you one
or two more reactions from Cooper:

Today [April 1848, in a letter to his wife] J. J.
Astor goes to the tomb... Irving is an execu-
tor, and the report says with a legacy of
$50,000. What an instinct that man has for
gold! He is to be Astor's biographer! Columbus and John Jacob Astor. I dare say Irving
will make the last the greatest man.

All Cooper's comments were not negative, of course.
Cooper thought that Irving's *Sketch Book* was much his
best work and could not have been written without a
knowledge of Europe and here he is, in a sense, defending
both Irving and himself for their European residences
and travels.

In an 1850 letter to the printer, Cooper put Irving and
Paulding, "a few years my senior," he says, at the top of
the list of American writers and himself third. And then,
on second thought, he added that *Thanatopsis* by Bryant
stands at the head.

I think it's characteristic that Irving should have helped
Cooper at the beginning, in 1821, and should have presided
at the memorial service to Cooper at the very end. The
relationship between them, in short, strikes me plainly as
one of rivalry. Though Cooper was six years younger,

Irving's fame had come much earlier. Irving was almost universally well-liked. Cooper was, later on in his life, very widely disliked, and attacked in the press for his lawsuits and his prickly rectitude.

I think there was some envy of Irving's prosperity involved, and I'm much struck, you know, in putting these notes together, by a kind of puritanical quality in James Fenimore Cooper. This is all the more astonishing in view of the fact that he did not like the Puritans.

Irving's relationship to Poe was an extraordinarily interesting one. Irving was generous to Poe. Poe, of course, paid Irving the supreme tribute of imitating his work, and the *Journal of Julius Rodman,* for example, borrows very liberally from *Astoria.*

Irving liked Hawthorne more than Cooper or Poe, surely. He considered Hawthorne's writings as "among the very best that had ever been issued from the American Press," according to modern critic Newton Arvin. Hawthorne, in turn, introduced Irving at the top of his list of contemporary friends in the "Hall of Fantasy" naming Irving, Lowell, Emerson, Longfellow, Cooper, Allston and so forth, and then took their names out when he republished the *Mosses From an Old Manse.*

Some degree of private feeling may have been represented in one of his wife's letters. The Hawthornes, as you know, were immensely pleased at Melville's pseudonymous review of *Mosses,* and Sophia wrote her mother, "At last someone speaks the right word of Mr. Hawthorne. .. I have been wearied and annoyed hitherto with hearing him compared to Washington Irving and other American writers and put, generally, *second.*" Of course, in her secret mind, the right comparison was with Shakespeare.

Finally, in *A Wonder Book,* Hawthorne has his narrator, Eustace Bright, mention the story of Rip Van Winkle. The children want to hear it, of course, but the student replies that "The story had been told once already, and better than it ever could be told again." He insists that it would grow as old as "The Gorgon's Head" and other miraculous legends and it would last as long.

This is an extremely fine and grateful tribute, it seems to me, on Hawthorne's part.

Longfellow, we know, was a great admirer of Irving, knew him personally, and said, "Every reader has his first book." His first book was *The Sketch Book*.

Let's conclude with a brief discussion of Melville. Irving learned of Melville's *Typee*, his first book, through the publisher, Murray, and was enough interested to visit Gansevoort Melville, Herman's elder brother, in London, and to listen for an hour to passages of *Typee* which he read aloud from the proof sheets. He prophesied the book's success, and declared portions of it to be exquisite and the style graphic. This was in early 1846. A month later, Gansevoort showed the preface and the appendix to Irving, who "expressed himself highly pleased," and again said he was certain the book would be successful.

Melville very likely met Irving and others of the New York literary group through Evert Duyckinck, an editor and biographer, at the end of the 1840s. In 1847, Duyckinck was persuaded that Melville was modeling his writing a good deal on that of Washington Irving, especially in the satirical articles on Zachary Taylor. Even so, before *Pierre* and Melville's loss of audience and reputation, he seems mostly to have considered Irving a "mere grasshopper." (This is a phrase out of Newton Arvin's biography, and I have no other authority for it.) But after *Pierre*, when Melville turned to writing short tales for the first time in his career, for *Putnam's Magazine* and for *Harper's*, he seems to be working in the Washington Irving vein. *I And My Chimney* (1856) has some of the sunny, easy quaintness of Irving, along with "The Happy Failure," "The Fiddler," and "Jimmy Rose" (1854-1855).

I would suggest that Melville touches depths of pathos in these stories, not to be found in Irving, but the humor and ease and romantic melancholy, and the backward look are very much the same.

Melville's fullest sympathy with Irving came in his old

age, when he wrote the prose and poetry sketch, called "Rip Van Winkle's Lilac," and dedicated it to the happy shade of Washington Irving. In this piece, plainly, he feels tenderly about Irving, and about his own childhood countryside, his own childhood ambience. The lilac tree, of this sketch with its heavy trunk and its load of blossoms, which Van Winkle had planted when he was young, has furnished slips for dozens of other households and dooryards. It functions in the sketch as an emblem of fragrance and beauty and creativity. The sketch is unpolished. It is touched occasionally with sentimentality, but it is a very fine tribute, indeed, to Irving's qualities.

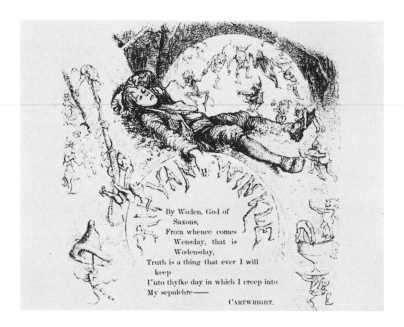

By Woden, God of
Saxons,
From whence comes
Wensday, that is
Wodensday,
Truth is a thing that ever I will
keep
Unto thylke day in which I creep into
My sepulchre——
CARTWRIGHT.

ILLUS. 13—*Rip Van Winkle by Augustus Hoppin*

BIBLIOGRAPHY

Bowers, Claude, *The Spanish Adventures of Washington Irving*. Boston: Houghton Mifflin, 1940.

Brooks, Van Wyck. *The World of Washington Irving*. New York: E. P. Dutton, 1944.

Butler, Joseph T. *Washington Irving's Sunnyside*. Tarrytown: Sleepy Hollow Restorations, 1968.

Hedges, William. *Washington Irving, An American Study, 1802-1832*. Baltimore: Johns Hopkins Press, 1965.

Hoffman, Daniel G. "Irving's Use of American Folklore in 'The Legend of Sleepy Hollow,'" *PMLA*, Vol. LXVIII, No. 3 (June 1953).

Irving, Pierre M. *The Life and Letters of Washington Irving*. 4 vols. New York: G. P. Putnam, 1862-1864.

Leary, Lewis. *Washington Irving*. Minneapolis: University of Minnesota Press, 1963. (University of Minnesota Pamphlets on American Writers, No. 25).

McClary, Ben Harris, ed. *Washington Irving and the House of Murray*. Knoxville: University of Tennessee Press, 1969.

Pochmann, Henry A., ed. *Washington Irving*: Representative Selections. New York: American Book Company, 1934.

Reichart, Walter A., *Washington Irving and Germany*. Ann Arbor: University of Michigan Press, 1957.

Wagenknecht, Edward. *Washington Irving: Moderation Displayed*. New York: Oxford University Press, 1962.

Williams, Stanley T. *The Life of Washington Irving*. 2 vols. New York: Oxford University Press, 1935.

Williams, Stanley T. *The Spanish Background of American Literature*. 2 vols. New Haven, Conn.: Yale University Press, 1955.

CONTRIBUTORS

JOSEPH T. BUTLER is Curator of Sleepy Hollow Restorations and has a Masters degree from both Ohio University and the University of Delaware (Winterthur Fellow). He is American Editor of *The Connoisseur* and has written and lectured extensively on the early American arts and on Irving.

WILLIAM M. GIBSON, Professor of English at New York University, was Director of the Center For Editions Of American Authors. In a distinguished career as scholar and teacher in American Literature, he has been awarded Fellowships under the Fulbright Program and from the Guggenheim Foundation and the American Council of Learned Societies.

WILLIAM L. HEDGES was Chairman of the English Department at Goucher College and has taught American Literature at Harvard, Wisconsin, and the University of California at Berkeley. His writings on Irving include "Washington Irving" in *Major Writers of America* and *Washington Irving: An American Study*.

HERBERT L. KLEINFIELD, Professor of English at C. W. Post Center of Long Island University, is Managing Editor of the ongoing *Complete Writings of Washington Irving* in which he is co-editor of the Letters. A consultant to the

Dictionary of American Biography, his scholarship on Irving includes "A Census of Washington Irving Manuscripts."

ANDREW B. MYERS is President of the Faculty Senate at Fordham University and Editorial Consultant to Sleepy Hollow Restorations. A Grolier Club Member and Fellow of the Pierpont Morgan Library, he is on the Board of Editors of the Irving Edition of which he is editing the Spanish Journals and co-editing *The Alhambra.*

LORMAN A. RATNER is Chairman of the Department of History at Lehman College of the City University of New York. A specialist in Cultural History, his writings have appeared in the major American historical journals and he is the Editor of *The American Historical Sources* series.

HASKELL S. SPRINGER is Assistant Professor of English at the University of Kansas. His graduate degrees are from Indiana University and he has taught American Literature at the University of Virginia. The author of articles on E. E. Cummings and W. D. Howells as well as Irving, he is editing *The Sketch Book* in the Irving Edition.

CARL H. WOODRING is Professor of English at Columbia University where he has been Chairman of the English Department. A distinguished scholar and teacher in English Romanticism, he has authored works on Coleridge and Wordsworth in particular. He is a member of the Executive Council of the Modern Language Association.

SYMPOSIA IN HONOR OF
WASHINGTON IRVING

The symposium from which the present volume derives is the first in what will become a series of, at least, biennial conferences on the life and works of Washington Irving, under the sponsorship of Sleepy Hollow Restorations, Inc. They will focus on the complex achievements of Washington Irving, as man of letters and as public figure, in an America which was rapidly expanding and intellectually maturing.

Sleepy Hollow Restorations

include

Sunnyside, the 19th century home of author Washington Irving in Tarrytown, New York.

Van Cortlandt Manor, a Revolutionary era estate in Croton-on-Hudson, New York.

Philipsburg Manor Upper Mills, an 18th century gristmill-trading center and residence complex in North Tarrytown, New York.

The three restorations, which span three centuries of Hudson River Valley history, are properties of **Sleepy Hollow Restorations, Inc.**, a non-profit educational corporation, made possible by the late John D. Rockefeller, Jr.

DATE DUE